The Golden Coast

BY HARNETT T. KANE

LOUISIANA HAYRIDE—
America's Rehearsal for Dictatorship

THE BAYOUS OF LOUISIANA

DEEP DELTA COUNTRY
(American Folkways Series)

PLANTATION PARADE

NATCHEZ ON THE MISSISSIPPI

NEW ORLEANS WOMAN
Biographical Novel of Myra Clark Gaines

BRIDE OF FORTUNE
Novel Based on the Life of Mrs. Jefferson Davis

QUEEN NEW ORLEANS
City by the River

PATHWAY TO THE STARS
Novel Based on the Life of John McDonogh

GENTLEMEN, SWORDS AND PISTOLS
Dueling in the South

THE SCANDALOUS MRS. BLACKFORD
Novel Based on the Life of Harriet Blackford, with Victor LeClerc

DEAR DOROTHY DIX
With Ella Bentley Arthur

THE LADY OF ARLINGTON
Novel Based on the Life of Mrs. Robert E. Lee

SPIES FOR THE BLUE AND GRAY

THE SMILING REBEL
Novel Based on the Life of Belle Boyd

MIRACLE IN THE MOUNTAINS
The Life of Martha Berry, with Inez Henry

THE GALLANT MRS. STONEWALL
Novel Based on the Lives of Gen. and Mrs. Stonewall Jackson

THE SOUTHERN CHRISTMAS BOOK

THE GOLDEN COAST

The Golden Coast

BY

Harnett T. Kane

PHOTOGRAPHS BY

James Ricau

DOUBLEDAY & COMPANY, INC.
GARDEN CITY, NEW YORK

Library of Congress Catalog Card Number 59-5367

Printed in the United States of America

Designed by Atkinson Dymock

To Mavis McIntosh,

WHO SUGGESTED THIS BOOK FOUR YEARS AGO

Contents

The Golden Coast

Texas mood: the dunes and the skies of Padre Island

Paradise

Discovered

IT is a land golden in several ways: brightly splashed for much of the year by a possessive sun; golden, too, in a tapestry of history and incident more highly colored than that of any other part of North America, and also in a vast wealth that is only beginning to pour out to the world.

The Gulf Coast of the United States reaches in an irregular crescent from the last island tip of Florida, past the sand beaches of Alabama and Mississippi and the marshy edges of Louisiana to the long, downthrust shore of Texas. Here is the America first discovered by Europeans a hundred years before the Pilgrims went to Massachusetts, and here the serene skies witnessed some of the bloodiest clashes that fixed a continent's destiny.

But this coast is, at the same time, a frontier—America's final one. For centuries most men passed over the wide arc as an isolated waste.

Today the ground along the surging blue of the Gulf of Mexico draws millions of people who help to open it as a great "new" region with an incalculable future, a natural treasure as yet largely untapped.

In another fashion the coast is entering the nation's consciousness. A farspread playground has come into being, a series of play areas of a haunting beauty of lake and island and vivid bloomings. Its edges reach within a hundred miles of the tropics, with bougainvillaea, flame vine and oleander rising yellow and scarlet and purple against a background of ripe profusion. Tens of thousands arrive here regularly to relax, then return to settle as new residents.

It is in the South, yet not precisely of the South. In some parts lines of columned houses extend for miles with high galleries like those of Charleston or Natchez or New Orleans' Garden District, but in many respects the Gulf Coast is a "foreign" area of America, occupied by people of a warmer, more vivid culture than that of the Anglo-Saxon. The region touches closely upon the Latin lands, is dominated here and there by a French civilization and spotted by other Southern and Central European additions.

As a result it seems a place of the relaxed spirit, the calm assumption of any joys or cares that the day will bring. Its people know bright excitements, happy hours that they enjoy to the fullest, but they are well adjusted to life as they find it. In the words of a native: "Mister, we're just a take-it-easygoing bunch."

Only a short distance inland, at various points, men lead far different existences, more solemn, oriented to their immediate neighborhood. By contrast the coast has a maritime flavoring. Through the generations the coasters have sailed the Gulf for pleasure or for their support, and also looked toward the world beyond them.

Here are narrow islands strung like a woman's necklace along the shore; tranquil lagoons, expanses of grass that bend with the wind, crisscrossed by uncounted winding streams. Physically the Gulf area is the youngest part of the United States, for it remained open sea many centuries after the continent rose above the bottom. Only slowly did it lift, dripping from the ocean, to drop again before rising once more. Thousands of miles appear half completed, in an uncertain state between water and dry soil.

Here is the United States' closest approach to the Spanish world of Central America, which has influenced Gulf habits in a hundred ways: spiced food, a lingering taste for rest in the afternoon, and also for lively fiestas. To a greater degree than any other section of North

Full of years and full of life, in Louisiana

Light sands, dark eyes
on a Mississippi beach

In Alabama, "wherever you
can, you push out a pier" . . .

America, these shores have become a place of ceremonies, parades and general festivities.

As a New Englander-turned-Floridian said with a laugh: "These new neighbors of mine are always celebrating something or somebody. Last week I joined in a festival named for a pirate, and I'm sure my ancestors revolted in their graves."

And why not a pirate, like anybody else, the Gulf Coast man will inquire of you? The place has known priests and outlaws, martyrs and rascals, picaroons, swindlers and plain eccentrics, and like the tolerant land that it is, it has taken each on his own terms.

Through its story runs a thread of smuggling and related doings. Nature made the unending, tattered coast an inevitable scene of such operations. "Anybody a fool," a Louisiana marshman informed me, "if he don' use what he got—all these lil island' and twistin's o' water. Now ain' he?"

Generations of men have slipped in with forbidden silks, forbidden jewels, a world of other forbidden items. The coast has had wreckers who "assisted" dangerous reefs in drawing ships to their destruction —and also quiet individuals on remote stretches, who violated this or that law mainly because they never heard of it.

Still, to fool a government agent . . . that was a fine thing in the eyes of many an old-time coastman. "See that one? His *grand-grandpère* got rich by running things past the Federals." The remark is made not in criticism, but in tribute. From the ragged edges of Florida and Alabama and Mississippi to the bays below New Orleans and Galveston, Corpus Christi and other Texas points, each locality has its devious heroes.

Over the years, to fight other opponents as well as pirates, the various nations have given the Gulf forts that altered American history. Some helped change naval development, in clashes of armored vessels against wooden ones, ships against stone fortifications. Here occurred some of the first and also the last conflicts of the Confederacy, including one after the war closed with Lee and Grant at Appomattox. That scene took place, of course, in Texas.

The coast saw a progression of broken hopes, generations of heartbreak, as explorers hunted for gold, pearls and other booty that was not there. Later settlers arrived with different dreams or schemes, and gambled on ventures that hung by a thread. One spot after another invited plungers with ideas that made others gape: a "seagoing railroad" across open water and sand spits down to America's farthest island-town; a reproduction of a Venetian palace of a sort that the

Deepest South: play hour
at Bahia Hondo on the Florida Keys

Sentinels: line of cabbage palms in Lower Rio Grande Valley

doges never conceived; a fifty-mile canal to make a world port out of inland Houston; islands dredged out of lakes; cities whose location was determined by consultation with "pixies" or little unseen men.

At times the enterprises worked handsomely; again they sank away, leaving abandoned "castles" and paved avenues moving past nothing to nowhere in the grass. In the meantime this has been the land of Ponce de Leon and Thomas Edison, of Jean Lafitte and Ben ("the Beast") Butler; of Admiral Farragut, who damned the torpedoes at Mobile, and the French Government's "casket girls" who brought much-needed femininity to the deprived men of colonial times.

It has been the land of the Confederacy's Judah Benjamin, who figured in a suspense tale of escape from the wreckage of one life to the beginning of another across the ocean. It is the coast, too, of Jesse Jones of Texas and Florida's Ringling Brothers, Barnum and Bailey; of Mississippi's Jefferson Davis, and, not least, of men who survive in life by wrestling alligators or pulling moss from trees.

Now, as in the early days, this can be a place of vast placidity, a pastoral, fragrant one of salt tang, the bitter-sweet smell of oleander upon the sands. At many a point a man can be as alone as on an island in the Atlantic. A little later he can make his way about quiet back lanes with wooden houses like those of small European settlements, and find roads that meander in casual Gulf style. When such a street approaches a rare old oak in its path, it simply curves to the side. For efficient strangers who think that odd, the coast man has a question: "What else would you do, eh?"

My first sight of the coast came when I was six and the family spent a week or so with friends near Pass Christian in Mississippi. Like any city boy I enjoyed the slow lap of the waters, the dots of distant islands against the sun, the whisperings of treasure cached beneath the wet sands.

Above all there was the first hour of sunset when the blazing disc approached the horizon, painting shore and pale walls and the faces around us with a golden light. Across the clouds an irregular line of birds skimmed down, then swung upward with hoarse cries. Here was and still is a paradise of brilliant birds, in regular congregation or in passage between the continents, with the freshness of the waves like an invitation from another land. The yellow light that came just before dusk . . . It is a memory of the Gulf to which I always return.

Early and late I learned, however, that it can be a cruel place, out of which deadly winds roar down, thrusting mountains of relentless water on houses and people. In this area have occurred some of the great disasters of America. The hurricane threat has not yet been defeated; still, despite setbacks, the Gulf population is learning how to cope with it—at least to leave remote outposts before the blow strikes.

Meanwhile the Gulf folk have come slowly to understand the astonishing wealth that lies below them. Today riches all but explode from the terrain in one of the major industrial advances of modern America. From the soil and the coastal waters that lie beyond it, millions of barrels of oil are spurting. Great pillars of salt, enormous chunks of sulphur, lime and related chemical materials fill the earth along the Louisiana-Texas littoral.

Pipelines cover miles of the earth, with rigs and storage tanks, drillers and countless types of other equipment, from Orange, Beaumont, Port Arthur and Houston down toward Corpus Christi and Brownsville. For generations to follow, America's largest single industry, oil, will center here, and many others will cluster about it.

Along the Mississippi in the area of New Orleans, and on Houston's borders, spectacular industrial complexes are lighting the skies, changing the scene about them. Great new shipbuilding surges ahead, near military and Navy establishments of a size never imagined in earlier days. But next to these shiny structures stand older towns, several among America's most ancient, with populations that have altered as little as have their settlements.

Within an hour's travel, or less, of New Orleans or Lake Charles, Louisiana, a visitor hears four or five languages, a half dozen accents: the staccato speech of a bayou dweller, the softness of a Sicilian dialect, the husky talk of a "Tacko" from Yugoslavia. Hands rise in gesture, voices break, there are many lifts of the shoulder, much smiling, in the manner of the more expressive races. And the Gulf man explains: "All these new thing', they come, and we take 'em and change 'em a lil, to be like us. Tha's all."

The modern ways arrive, and the coasters accept them on their own terms and go on being much the same as they always were.

The GOLDEN COAST

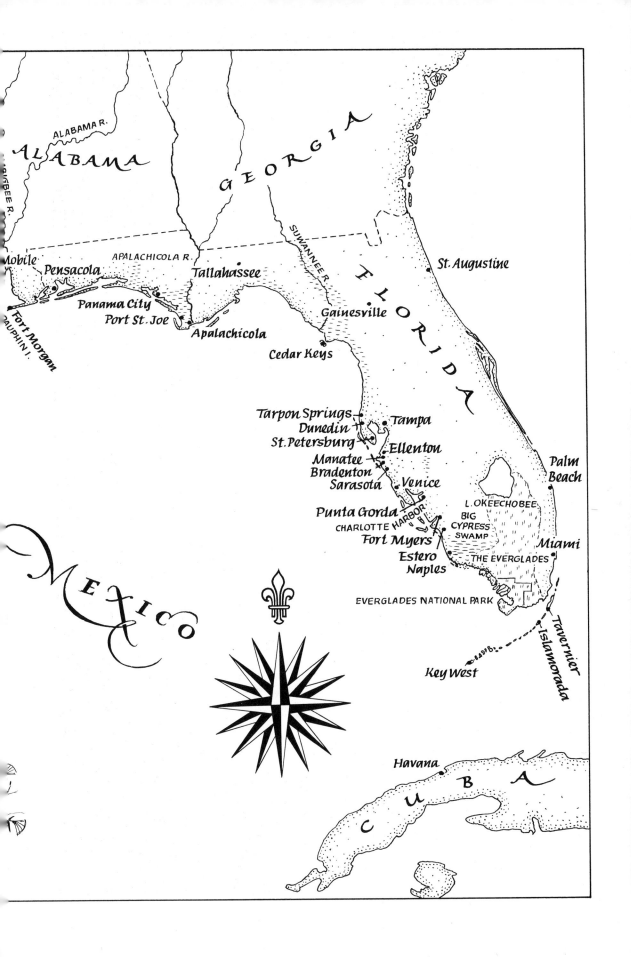

Pensacola: pattern in brick, arches, and sunlight

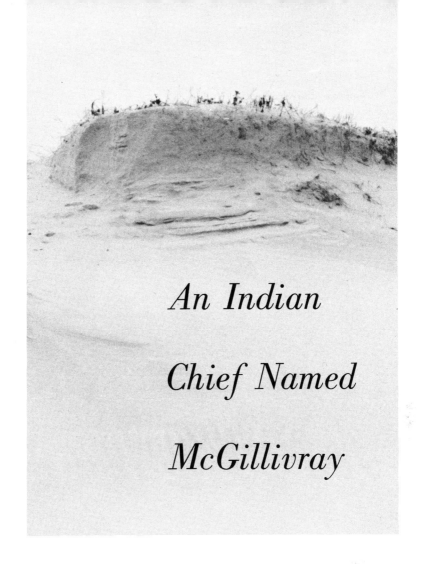

An Indian Chief Named McGillivray

i

THE oldest of all Gulf settlements is Pensacola. It has also been, in a clear sense, the most popular, because practically everybody in sight wanted to take it and, at one time or another, did. The things that happened to this busy town of western Florida have happened, I think, to no other place in North America.

Thirteen times the Pensacolians shifted owners; during one period they had a new master four times in four months. As a number of observers said, they changed flags as often as some people changed neckties. Understandably visitors noticed a certain "restlessness" among the old-time natives.

Nobody who lived among or near the Pensacolians illustrates so well the complexity of their life as Alexander McGillivray, who, his name notwithstanding, was chief of the Creek Indians of the nation above Pensacola. The world has known Scots-Irishmen, Scots-Englishmen and many another Scots mixture, but Alexander was a Scots-Indian. His father came from Scotland, his mother from America—the union of a Frenchman and an Indian. Alexander was educated by a Presbyterian minister-uncle; as chief he was bowed to by governors and honored by George Washington. He also showed versatility by serving (at high pay) as an officer in the armies of Britain, Spain and the United States, sometimes when two or more of the countries were in active enmity. This Mr. McGillivray, it may be submitted, was an adaptable man, and also as canny as a Scotsman is supposed to be.

First, the beginnings of Pensacola and the coast. Nearly a century before the earliest known Europeans felt their way along the Hudson, the Gulf shores saw pioneer white men. For most of that century the area was the major focus of their interest, with the beautifully located deep-water bay of Pensacola as a point of special attention.

Juan Ponce de Leon of Spain reached the Gulf in 1513. Eventually millions would seek rejuvenation in Florida, but the tale that this virile individual went mainly on a hunt for a Fountain of Youth was concocted later. Ponce de Leon sought one thing: wealth in any form. Reaching the Atlantic, he sailed Florida's long coast, like the outline of a downpointing finger; rounding the finger's end, he continued up the Gulf and halted near present-day Tampa or Charlotte Harbor.

For days Ponce de Leon stayed at the tranquil locale, with its thick mangroves on stiltlike roots and the feathery fronds of palms that stirred in the wind. But the Indians of Florida had already heard about the *conquistadores* who brought civilization to the benighted New World islands, along with murder, rape and torture. In a bloody fight several red men died and also a Spaniard; the Gulf Coast may therefore claim the first of countless white men killed in the area of the United States.

Piqued, the Spaniards left. Ponce de Leon could not, however, forget a few bits of gold that he had seen—not very good gold, but still gold. A few years later he was back, to receive arrows and a fatal wound. Pánfilo de Narváez, Hernando de Soto and others found storms, fevers, Indians and other mishaps; starving, they ate acorns and roots, their own horses and Florida grasses, and in the end each died or staggered away, to wander on as wrecks of men. They always grasped for gold that was not there, until 1559, when Spain at last made a serious effort to colonize rather than exploit the Gulf.

For a large-scaled venture she chose the matchless harbor that her men had often noted, Pensacola. Fifteen hundred people crowded the sands under the direction of the well-to-do, ambitious and, unfortunately, stupid Tristan de Luna. American history, beginning at Pensacola, might have been different had the leader been another kind of man.

It was fall, a season when Gulf Coasters later learned to keep one eye on the clouds. The newcomers cowered before the crashing force of a hurricane. De Luna had neglected to move their badly needed food and supplies to land, and the storm wiped out practically all their ships. These first Pensacolians went hungry, had furious disputes, met disastrous experiences among the red men as they moved helplessly about. Within two years the colony had ended. Yet Pensacola could claim a place as the first colony founded within the borders of the United States, and in 1959 it will celebrate what it calls "America's first quadricentennial."

Although there was enormous potential wealth around Pensacola and the coast, the Europeans were blind to it. The Spanish King ordered a stop to efforts in the region; for a century and a quarter it lay forgotten while Spain gave her attention to the Atlantic side and to St. Augustine, founded in 1565. White birds swung over the empty Gulf beaches and the thousands of green-hung islands and lagoons. Only a threat from France made Spain go back.

The French were moving all too actively down the powerful Mississippi, not far from western Florida, and in 1698 the court dispatched a new band to Pensacola. This one clung with determination—a virtue that many future Pensacolians were to require. Soon afterward a small French party rode to the mouth of the bay. They were hunting pirates, Canadian ones, they said.

To the Pensacolians this had a suspicious sound, and they refused to let the French enter. Sailing off, the new arrivals put up their own settlements at Biloxi and Mobile, the latter only sixty miles away. Nervously the Spaniards protested; that was all *their* land, *señors*. Politely the French listened at Mobile and stayed. Nevertheless, the two colonies got on pleasantly enough. Pensacola dozed in the sun, with a wooden fort named San Carlos after the King, a collection of palmetto-thatched huts and little more. Drill or labor in the morning, siesta in the afternoon, songs and wine after dark . . . An early pattern was set.

Twenty years later Spain and France went to war. Spanish Pensacola was slow in learning the news, but French Mobile was not. On a bright afternoon the Pensacolians saw a French force before them, and heard the demand: "Surrender!" The pleasant days had ended. Having little choice, the Pensacola garrison gave way—provided the invaders would send them to Spain's nearest city, Havana. The French agreed, and dispatched them south in French ships under a flag of truce.

Now came comedy, though the participants might not have described it as that. A Spanish fleet intercepted the party, snatched it up, and sent it right back to Pensacola with Spaniards in charge. Surrender, said the Spanish leaders. This time the guns were in the other hands, and the French were the ones to give way.

Over in their town of Mobile, the other French heard what had happened, and it was their turn to be irked. A new expedition, a French one, sailed toward Pensacola, and the two sides poured their fire across the sand and water. The French won, let their Indian allies conduct a zestful tomahawk raid, set fire to the settlement and stayed on to watch over the wreckage. Glumly the Spaniards, or those who survived, left the scene.

Less than six months later France and Spain made peace in Europe, and by treaty Pensacola returned to Spain. The Spaniards came over, and it was the French who left. There followed Pensacola's first period of serenity, a whole forty years. More drills in the morning, more siestas, more wine . . . until yet another war broke out. This time France and Spain, no longer enemies, united against England.

England won, and took Pensacola with all the rest of the Gulf Coast extending to the Mississippi river. At Pensacola most of the Spaniards said good-bye. As a native declared: "This was a place where people were *always* coming and going." Far different owners from the old ones, the British went to work in 1763 to create a new town with a new accent. They cleared marshes, laid out streets, built bigger houses; they launched farming on a large scale with imported slaves, and Pensacola flourished for the first time.

Names like Carlos, customs like the afternoon rest disappeared. With streets called after King George and Queen Charlotte, Pensacola became a semitropic version of an English waterside town, but with lingering Spanish overtones. As capital of British West Florida, it was the center of a soaring Indian trade, and a firmly Tory town.

Up along the Atlantic coast doughty Anglo-Saxons were rebelling against rule from England. British Pensacolians had little sympathy with such rude goings-on, and when thousands of Tory colonists fled the anger of the American patriots, many headed here. One took rank as the town's first famous figure, the shrewd William Panton, hailed by Pensacolians as the "first millionaire" within borders of the United States.

The quiet-working, untalkative Mr. Panton proved that a man could fill his pockets in this land. Taking furs and other salable objects from the red men, he paid them in the best calico, guns and generous fistfuls of beads. But Panton could not have succeeded as he did without the help of his silent partner, Alexander McGillivray, the Scots-Indian.

Alexander's father, a Scotsman of good family, had been an Indian trader who accumulated his own large estate. Eventually he developed an interest beyond barter with the Indians, marrying Sehoy Marchand, whose mother was an important Creek, her father a French captain. The boy grew up slim and handsome, with sharp, dark eyes and a restrained manner. Alexander's first thirteen or fourteen years were spent among his mother's people in the Creek nation; then his father sent him to Charleston to be tutored in highly un-Indian style by his preacher-uncle.

Returning to the Creeks, Alexander advanced steadily until he reached a height achieved by none of his predecessors, as dominant chief of the nation. He enjoyed all the privileges of two races; he had a plantation with Negro slaves, and separate establishments in which he maintained at least three wives.

Here was hardly a traditional red man. Alexander never claimed to be a fighter, though he sometimes permitted or encouraged his followers to go on the warpath. Yet he took no part in the hallooing and scalp-hunting; a brother-in-law told how Alexander once agreed to support a battle with the Americans, but only gingerly. Taking off his clothes, as everybody expected him to do, the Scots-Indian smeared himself with paint—then went into the bushes to await results. The fight over, Alexander darted out, quivering with cold, and snatched a coat from one of the white men's corpses. He himself chuckled over the incident.

McGillivray was notable, however, for his handling of men in council and at the negotiation table. He organized the Creeks as they had never been organized; from the whites he gained more, for himself and his people, than any other had received. He lived at a period when, if he and his people were to survive the plotting whites, he had to be as cunning as they.

And so . . . The rebellious American colonists had been harsh with his loyalist father, and Alexander sided with the Tories, receiving pay as an English colonel. When the Spaniards came to power near him, he made a deal with them and joined the Spanish payroll; eventually he did the same thing with the Americans.

Some frowned upon McGillivray for his course. For them he had a simple answer: An Indian took presents from any man who offered them. He served always, and served well, a people besieged by greedy whites. And he worked loyally with his fellow of Scottish heritage, the merchant Panton, who set up a great trading post at Pensacola. Each man proved himself an internationalist of a sort.

Changes were in the making for them and for Pensacola. Spain had never given up her liking for the area. When England was heavily occupied with the troublesome Americans, the Spanish Governor Galvez of Louisiana took advantage of the situation to send a strong force against the port. After eighteen years of British rule, the Pensacolians surrendered as they had done so many times before. Obediently the flagbearer trotted out with the old flag, and the town went Spanish for another forty years.

The returning masters changed the British-sounding main street from George to Pala Fox, and added others like Zarragossa, Barcelona and Tarragona. Back came the siesta, a taste for occasional gaming, and an intensified Latin look, with stuccoed houses, courtyards and grilled balconies in the Spanish manner. Yet some things continued more or less British, among them the Scotsman Panton. The Spaniards wanted the Indian trade, which Panton and McGillivray had tied up with a thousand strands; to keep it, they kept Panton, even waiving their usual requirement of an oath of full allegiance. Trade, if not love, conquers everything . . .

As the Spanish watched uneasily, the Americans made strong overtures to the Creeks, and the Scots-Indian came still further to the fore. McGillivray led a band to New York, where President Washington and his associates worked hard to please them. On his way McGillivray became a celebrity, smiled at, deferred to. With the United States he made an agreement over disputed lands, with a secret commission for himself, as a brigadier.

The chief, however, had been a sick man for a long time, suffering from a variety of ailments which included somewhat un-Indian-sounding headaches that put him to bed for days. He fell ill and died at Panton's house in Pensacola.

After McGillivray the Creeks managed far less well, and eventually broke into furious fighting with the Americans, to their own harsh loss. By now the people of the new nation were pushing steadily southward. When the United States took all of Louisiana at a bargain-counter sale, the pressure against the Florida Spaniards grew stronger by the month.

Some Americans considered the land an enormous bog and nothing more. In the words of John Randolph, Virginian: "No man would emigrate to Florida—no, not from hell itself." Many others disagreed, and land-hunting *Americanos* rapped heavily at Spain's Florida doors. At Pensacola the ever-weakening rulers received, among others, a mixed band whose activities disturbed the Anglo-Saxons in the regions bordering Florida: runaway slaves, Indians of shadowy connections and, not least, British spies.

The United States was approaching its second war with England, and Pensacola seemed a bed of intrigue aimed at the Americans. A certain peppery Army commander, Andrew Jackson, did not like the smell of the place. More and more, he fretted, the Indians were being stirred against the Americans. All at once Jackson had still more to disturb him.

A British expedition sailed into Pensacola to fortify it. (The theoretically neutral Spaniards made mild complaints, and that was all.) English officers went to work in proper British style to drill and march the Indians in red coats. One observer laughed; they "might as well have attempted to train the alligators of the Florida lagoons . . ." Overnight two flags flew together over the town: Spanish and British. Even for Pensacola this was something new!

Officially the United States was at peace with Spain, but that did not deter the forthright Jackson. Whatever his government thought, he marched into Spanish territory, stormed Pensacola, and the English withdrew. So did Jackson, with another place in his mind—New Orleans, where he had a rendevzous with the British, and with fortune. After Jackson won, Pensacola and the rest of Spanish Florida were doomed to slow capture. The Americans blustered, demanded, elbowed their way about the border. When Indian raids, with Spanish approval, continued to disturb the frontiersmen, their commander, Jackson, acted again. If the Spaniards couldn't keep order in their own territory, he snapped, he'd do it *for* 'em!

He did. Without the consent of his government, the tight-lipped Andrew beat his way down into Pensacola again. The ever-active flagman came out to lift the brisk American banner. The Spaniards protested in outrage, and still Jackson stayed for months. Finally he withdrew, but returned proudly a few years later, as first American governor of the territory. After years of moiling, of revolution in the disputed areas, Spain ceded Florida to the upstart country.

And were the Pensacolians overjoyed at the change that made them American? Most of them could only groan as they watched the strange nation take over. Nor were some of the newcomers pleased at the things they saw. Rachel Jackson, for instance, shook her head when she noted how untypically American was this place of many mixtures.

Pensacola of 1821 had a gumbo of fishermen, Indians, Negroes, West Indians, workers and planters of a dozen national combinations, who acted like the natives of any Latin settlement. Merrymaking on Sunday, games of chance, open stores . . . Jackson tore down gambling places, shut up shops, and Rachel wrote rapturously: "Fiddling and dancing not heard any more on the Lord's day . . . Cursing not heard. What, what has been done in one week!"

The Jacksons went away, and the fiddling, dancing and gaming (if not the cursing) resumed; Pensacolians remained easygoing Gulf people. Americans crowded in, setting out new streets and houses, building an ever heavier cotton trade. Wagons and oxcarts lumbered up, piled high with cotton bales and also sugar barrels. Tallahassee, the new capital that lay about thirty miles from the Gulf, took on a character it never lost—a leisured air, white houses with pillars and hitching posts before the lawns. Sugar, Louisiana's staple, proved profitable at other places along the coast. And Pensacola's connection with slavery gave rise to a grim incident.

Jonathan Walker served in Florida as a cog in the "underground railroad" that helped Negroes escape to freedom. In 1844 he gathered seven refugees in a sailboat for a daring eight-hundred-mile run to the British Bahamas. They made the long passage down the coast, and around the Florida Keys, before they were captured.

At Pensacola raging Floridians tried to lynch Walker; there he awaited trial for months. Found guilty, he was placed in a pillory, given a sentence and the letters S.S., for Slave Stealer, burned with a red-hot brand in the palm of his hand. For men who sympathized with Walker the letters were a sign of honor. Many years later a Navy chaplain placed on his grave a monument showing the marked hand, and John Greenleaf Whittier used the incident for a celebrated poem.

Soon after the Americans took over, they recognized in Pensacola a place that might save the country in wartime. They built a Navy yard and eventually four strong forts that ringed the area: Pickens, McRae and Barrancas to guard the harbor entrance from attack by water, and Redoubt as protection from assault by land. For years

The Navy's been looking over Pensacola for a long, long time

Pickens, on Santa Rosa Island, was one of the two or three largest American forts; its construction, with "bent brick," feather-edging and "arches within arches," has amazed builders of today. Captain William Chase of the Army Engineers directed the work. The walls were from five to sixteen feet thick. When war broke with the North, the Confederates captured the Navy yard and other three forts, but not Pickens, to which the Union quickly shifted its forces.

Ironically William Chase found himself in command of the Southerners, who mounted a strong, vigorous attack on Fort Pickens. He must have realized, wryly, how well he had done his work; he could never breach the defenses. For nearly a year Pensacola had still another in the long line of banners that floated over it, the Stars and Bars, until the South gave up the port. At the war's end Pensacola suffered as trade dropped and sand drifted over empty streets. An ironic editor objected to the removal of weeds; they were, he said, the only things growing around the place.

In time, however, other things grew, and better days came back. The area saw the swift use of the towering pine and cypress that covered the terrain for many miles. In the 1890s an outlander counted nearly one hundred square-rigged ships taking lumber in the port. The harbor was extended, new shoreland created, and Pensacola sent its produce to the world.

Yet, again, slack days. The government lost interest in Pensacola as a naval site, and the town dragged along until 1914 when it gained the nation's attention in a new way. It was here, as the natives put it, that the American Navy first took wings. A little band of nine officers and less than twenty-five men arrived to change history with flimsy planes that looked like tin toys glued with wax. Watching, thousands were caught by the wonder of the strange "aerial machines" and the glamorous, begoggled figures who swept into the Gulf skies.

At Pensacola, through the war and afterward, the country nursed an infant that leaped to maturity. For nearly a quarter century this *was* the Navy in the air, and fields spread and spread again. Pensacola's past was linked with its present when, in draining for new air-landing space, government men dragged up massive logs which had been dropped there during the Confederate war to keep them from Northern hands. This time nobody objected when they went North for the restoration of "Old Ironsides."

With World War II Pensacola became a phenomenal spot, which sent forth almost thirty thousand airmen versed in the new

Mortar at Fort Barrancas:
short, fat, and murderous

technique of carrier attacks that had much to do with American victory. Its role in the war was a proud one, its achievements notable. Today the shadow of the jet age hangs over the town as thousands of men in uniform hang about its streets. For a large part of the population the "Navy Air" is the great economic fact of life—that and the other sea-connected callings that have been here for many generations. New industries, chemical and related plants, have sprung up in recent years, and the town works to diversify itself. Yet it remains tied to its Gulf.

Hundreds of Pensacolians leave regularly in ships to hunt for the huge, sixty-pound-or-heavier red snappers that wait out in the Gulf, and return many days later with their catch. Boats and ships skim in and out of the channel, and the waves that sometimes pound its long beaches do not let the town forget its kinship with the sea.

Here and there a Spanish air survives, with a suggestion of the ironwork and balconies of another civilization. Pensacolians point: "Here's where the British governors met with the Indian chiefs." "Mr. Panton's trading post was right there." This is Plaza Ferdinand VII, where troops drilled, and in the distance stand the remains of old Fort San Carlos, often torn down, often rebuilt, with a crumbling staircase, walls and gun tracks.

A short way off, Fort Barrancas sits on top of its hill with the supporting columns of its drawbridge still in place in the dry moat. On each side of the entrance there remains some of the machinery which operated the drawbridge, and beyond that its fine brickwork and granite block passages. A thousand yards back in the woods is Fort Redoubt, so well camouflaged with earthwork that a stranger may be startled when he comes upon the outer wall of the battle-scarred fortification. Over the bay, Fort McRea has gone underwater, a victim of the tides. And across the mile-wide entrance, among the dunes, stands Fort Pickens, the fortification that defied its builder.

Here, as elsewhere, the Latin element is strong among some of the whites and Negroes as well; a number of the latter tell proudly of their Spanish blood.

"This place," a tan-skinned man told me, "she bin a lil meltin' pot for true. My mama, she say *we* come from kings. I disremember which ones, though." He sighed. "The town sure seen plenty. Yeah, four hun'red years since the first folks come. . . . Sometimes it feel' like ever' bit of it."

Both of us jumped as a trio of jets streaked by. Among its oleanders and camellias, part of Pensacola retains its half-yawning air of the past, while the other part roars into the future. Leaving the townsman, I sought the resting place of Alexander McGillivray, the Indian chief who shivered while his followers did the fighting, but who led them better than any other of his times. It is marked by a tablet a short way from the crumbled chimney left from the warehouse of his friend, Mr. Panton. With all its upsets and its oddities of history, Pensacola produced no livelier figure than the Scots-Indian.

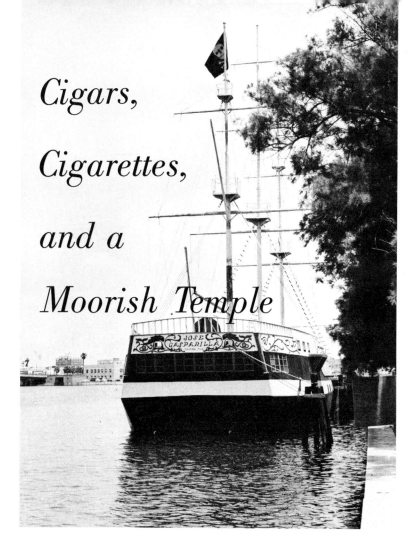

Cigars, Cigarettes, and a Moorish Temple

ii

DOWN the coast, Tampa and its environs are as new as Pensacola is old, but often they hide this newness. Recently I picked up a much-thumbed volume of 1912 which called Tampa "one of the most foreign-appearing cities in the United States." In certain places the statement still holds true.

Until late in the last century, much of the Tampa area consisted largely of wet grass, alligators and pelicans. It might have much the same status today except for several accidents. Tampa became what it is because of tobacco, Cuban revolutions, and a hard-minded Yankee who found it a rare place to fish for dollars.

For several hundred years the broad stretch of the Gulf had been unknown to the outer world. The very early Spanish explorers had touched here, noted the wide, protected harbor, and then forgotten it. Scattered fisherfolk, Indians, a pirate or two, men who started crops and gave up . . . these came and went until 1823, when the newly arrived American government put up a log fort with a stockade. A minute settlement straggled along, while Fort Brooke existed chiefly as a source of supply for the Indian Wars.

Schooners rode in and out, and a mixed, male crew clustered about the bay in tents and palmetto huts. This became a "cow country," with vessels carrying heavy loads of small Florida cattle to Cuba. Florida had its own "Cracker cowboys," and many laughed over the meager, tick-infested animals, "no bigger than a donkey," but in time a major industry was in the making.

The Indian wars ended, Fort Brooke was abandoned, and the Tampa settlement dozed along. Then and later the Tampans turned their eyes south toward Havana. During the war with the North the spot became a center for Southern cotton-running to Cuba, until Union forces blockaded and seized it. After the conflict Tampa sagged, until Henry Plant came along like a wizard with a wand.

Florida would hardly be the same today had it not been for two rival railroad tycoons who descended upon it in the 1880s. Both Henry Plant, Tampa's foster father, and Henry M. Flagler were originally from Connecticut; they had pushed themselves up the hard but well-paid way in a period when men of iron will could rule their worlds with a free hand. And both, as Marjory Stoneman Douglas observed, made fortunes by endless labor, tight fists and "the ability to see an available dollar through a slit no bigger than a gnat's eye."

Flagler took the East Coast of Florida, Plant the West, and they contested with flamboyant gestures. Although Henry Plant had occupied himself abroad during the Confederate War, he came forth as a Southern-planter type with flowing hair, mustaches and grand manner. In the postwar years he caught up bargains in declining Southern railroads for his "Plant System," part rail lines, part express company, part steamboat and steamship lines.

The two entrepreneurs had their gaze fixed upon the lush potential markets of Central and South America. They needed terminal points on the coast, and Flagler chose one spot after another, including one called Miami. As part of his game of boom, Flagler set up vast hotels to draw Easterners to his localities. In St. Augustine he planned his Ponce de Leon caravansary, dispatching two architects to Spain for some two years to collect ideas. The outcome was a gigantic structure in "Spanish Renaissance" style, plus Italian touches—many courts and towers and fountains, arched gateways left and right, and "450 sleeping apartments." Here were the beginnings of that national phenomenon known as Florida hotel building.

Whatever Flagler could do, Plant decided he could do better. Surveying the West Coast, the tycoon picked the harbor of Tampa for his port, pushing his lines out to it, and the town almost burst with excitement and pride. The story is that Plant sent a wire to Flagler, informing his competitor that his rails had reached tidewater at Tampa.

"Where is Tampa?" Flagler asked haughtily in reply.

"Just follow the crowds," Plant snapped.

The crowds were arriving. From a place with little more than seven hundred people, Tampa's population leaped to fifty-five hundred within five years, and before the next decade passed it touched fifteen thousand. By that time Plant had carried out a new scheme to put to shame Flagler's ornate inns at St. Augustine.

Nowhere else was there anything like Plant's Tampa Bay Hotel. One man stared at it and shook his head. "I don't believe it." It dominated the town, a wide, high pile that rises over the Florida flatlands like someone's fantasy. Flagler's Ponce de Leon inn covered one square; Plant's hotel two, with about twenty acres of ground. Like Flagler's architects, Plant's had resorted to Spain, not plain Spain but the Moorish sections.

Here was a florid version of a temple of the Moors, with bulbous minarets, silver domes and golden crescents. Wooden horseshoe designs and crescents had been nailed everywhere about the structure, five stories high in some sections, two in others, with cavernous halls, endless stone steps, piazzas the size of city streets, some twenty-six feet across. The walk outside extended precisely a mile, and all else was in proportion. Forests of oriental columns, Moorish pendants, a drawing room described as "a casket of antique things" . . . Mr. and Mrs. Plant had scoured Europe and picked up objects to scatter here and there.

The great mass cost an estimated three million dollars, an amount which bought far more then than now, and was spent in about twenty months. There was a purpose in the project; Plant hoped to capture the imagination, and the purses, of fashionable America of that Victorian day.

His opening night in 1891 brought a great splash. Two thousand guests—totaling a third of the town's whole population—arrived, and they included princes, dukes, duchesses, a marquis or two, Wall street figures, senators, writers who had "names." Opera singers gave solos and duets above the din of popping corks, and visitors rode about the grounds in rickshaws, admiring the palmettos, oranges

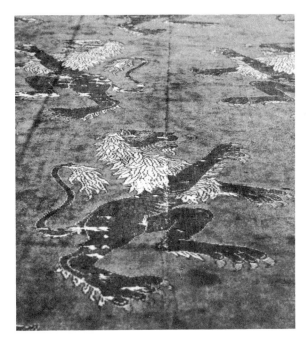

From hotel to university:
Mr. Plant wanted it Moorish

and pines, the glitter of the Florida-Moorish giant in the nearby waters.

Guests sniffed orange blossoms and growing pineapples, gaped at massive doors of Spanish mahogany, divans from the Tuileries, an oil portrait of Louis XIV, Japanese vases, German canvases and busts of such well-known people as Queen Elizabeth and Mary of the Scots. (Mr. Plant had branched out from the Moors.) And everywhere was the wonder of the fabulous new invention, the unshaded electric bulb, illuminating minarets, Mary of Scotland, and chairs on which Marie Antoinette had once sat.

Mr. Plant's largesse had its effect. Americans began to flock to Tampa, and other structures mushroomed. Railroad lines lengthened, warehouses grew, and everybody smiled when Mr. Plant appeared. Then, unexpectedly, arrived the town's blessing Number 2, the cigar.

Years earlier, cigar making had come to Key West, at the tip of the Florida Keys, from nearby Cuba. Eventually the people of the island raised the banners of revolt against their Spanish masters; when Spain retaliated, thousands made the short transfer to Key West. The volatile Cubans liked the freedom they found in America, but not the tragically low wages. Dissension broke out and in 1886, when a bad fire wiped out half of Key West, the cigar manufacturers seized their chance to move.

On a damp flat east of Tampa a "little Cuba" sprang up, with row after row of wooden shacks that took the name of Ybor City, after a leading cigar maker. The Cuban and Spanish elements provided a new base for the city's spreading growth. More and more men and women came up from Havana, and the Cuban look intensified, with churches, clubs and shops, tile roofs, stucco walls, ironwork and small courts.

The excitable newcomers often had a hard existence, but they enjoyed their frequent fiestas, their games in the style of their earlier homes. They maintained a warm feeling for their troubled fellows back in Havana. In the 1880s and '90s the movement for Cuban freedom flamed ever higher, and Tampans gave hot approval. Revolutionary agents visited Ybor City, held meetings in dimly lighted halls and about the patios. *"À dios!" "Cuba libre"* . . . The murmurs sounded in the night.

Then, in the early 1890s, New Orleans saw the brutal lynchings of Italians in a bloody "Mafia incident" for which the United States government apologized and paid indemnities. As a consequence, many Italians left the Creole city and these settled in and about

Tampa. They were largely Sicilians and Sardinians; in time the area had the Gulf Coast's greatest Latin concentration.

Overnight in 1898 Tampa broke into American fame. The *Maine* blew up in Cuban waters; war became certain and Tampa emerged as the embarkation point for thirty thousand or more Americans, its name a shouted byword. The Army command moved about Mr. Plant's Moorish replica, while the soldiers went elsewhere. Near makeshift camps the boys established friendly relations with the Cubans, including the Cuban girls, of Ybor City. And thousands of Tampans signed up to fight for their former country against Spain.

The town knew the swaggering Richard Harding Davis, who had a few words for it: "sand-blighted, squalid." Tampa also knew Colonel Theodore Roosevelt of the volunteer Rough Riders, who found the whole situation a glorious foul-up. Nobody met his men on their arrival; nobody had an idea where anybody was supposed to be or supposed to go, which vessels to board or where to locate them. At last Roosevelt's Riders reached their transport—and waited in it for a week in the broiling sun. Later, when the colonel wrote effervescently of his Rough Riders and the war, the humorist, Mr. Dooley, suggested a title: "Alone in Cubia."

The hostilities over, Tampa still spread itself, as the industrial and shipping point for most of West Florida. Eventually it could claim rank as the world's largest canner of citrus, as the producer of America's major supply of clear Havana cigars, and the area's chief business center.

In the Florida boom of the 1920s Tampans raced to cut new streets and put up new houses. One citizen, D. P. Davis, worked up a venture to create a brand-new island in the bay by digging up sand from the bottom. Mr. Davis set a fall date of 1924 for the sale of lots that were still largely in the water. The previous night hundreds stood in line for hours. Every lot was soon sold, double-sold and many triple-sold, with sellers claiming gains in the tens of thousands. Mr. Davis counted profits of millions, went on to a similar East Coast project—and met the crash. With only a fragment of his earnings left, he started for Europe and disappeared from the ship. Today, however, Davis Islands are places of subtropical beauty, with parkways, terraced lawns and many driveways, and Tampa has recovered from the broken boom.

The railroader Plant had also died; though he made Tampa, he never achieved his dream of establishing an elegant social center. His big Tampa Bay Hotel was, alas, all too big, a Moorish white elephant.

A visitor of 1917 thought her bedroom "like being in the Alhambra . . . furnished in the late Victorian manner." The empty dining room resembled "an Orientalized Pantheon, so astounding in its proportions that we entered in awe," their steps echoing around the great dome like the thunder of an army's movement. Arriving late for the evening meal, she estimated that three thousand electric bulbs lighted the dinner for two.

By then the hotel had become America's only municipally owned and operated one. Early in the twentieth century the Tampa Bay had gone to the city for less than $150,000. For years Tampa tried to decide what to do with it, until the newly formed University of Tampa took it on a long lease in 1933. Today boys and girls stroll past walls of dimming elegance; professors lecture in chambers that once echoed to arias from *Il Trovatore* and *Manon,* and inevitably students use a Venus' or Apollo's bare derrière for proclamations of election and the like.

"At first it was sort of funny to be in this place," a co-ed explained. "Now we never notice anything."

Tampa of the modern day is a place of contrasts between crowded industry and luxurious homes, between wind-swept boulevards and a grimly neglected Negro slum, the Scrub. Ybor City remains little changed by the years, a fringe of Havana in America, with houses in Cuban style, bright-eyed men and women with an air of the tropics —a semisomnolent place with a capacity to flare into instant excitement.

On my last visit old women whispered in Spanish, and young girls talked in slightly accented voices. An old man, sitting in dignity by himself, nodded as his grandson spoke: *"Sí, sí. Con mucho gusto. Sí . . ."* In a small circle of a garden a poinsettia stood limply, its red leaves drooping in the sun; among the shadows of a wide entryway several babies played together. A vendor sold newspapers in Spanish; ahead stood a movie house with a film in that language, and crowds moved in and out of various *centros* or clubs, organizations that look after the health and other needs of their people.

With friends I went to a tiled and mirrored restaurant, one of many in the area, that was reminiscent of those of Cuba or southern Spain. There I savored a superior *garbanzo* soup, a cold one of tomato, herbs and related items, and an aromatic casserole of rice with saffron, bits of chicken, fish, oysters, shrimp, and sausage. A small cup of ink-black coffee, and time arrived for a stroll.

On this early Sunday evening others had the same thought.

Tampa cigar plant: where tobacco is a fragrant king

Dozens of the young walked slowly along the streets while grand-mothers and grandfathers watched from inside. Soft laughter sounded from four girls in freshly starched dresses. "Ah, no. *No, no!*" One of them murmured the words half angrily, half amusedly, and we saw a group of boys approaching. Eyes met eyes or turned elaborately away; it was the old promenade, carried on much as in the older countries.

A moment later I sniffed: it was unmistakable, the smell of good tobacco that hangs over everything in this part of Tampa. It was a rich scent, suggestive of relaxed existence, of the quiet hour in the shade. The Latins of Tampa have many troubles, many uncertainties, but on such evenings, it seemed to me, they know a happier life than most others of the town.

A day later we went to one of the factories to see thousands of hands deftly at work. We watched "selectors" pick especially choice leaves and intent women as they shaped "royals," "coronas," "panatelas," "perfectos." "This is a *maduro*—dark, see?"—one gestured— "And a *claro claro,* very light. Oh, watch out for the *chabeta!*" The last was the knife used to cut the cigars. She smiled. "We make fine ones, you know. Haven't you heard that when they last had a king in Spain, one of our Tampa companies sold its cigars to him and his court?"

The man near her nodded proudly, and then his look became serious. "We had good days here once, better than now. Things were easier, not so many restrictions at the factory. Peddlers going around selling sweet stuff on sticks, and readers to keep the whole roomful interested as they worked." He shrugged. "Now, machines, more machines, and everybody on a stiff schedule, and not even a reader. They claimed those fellows read things that made us want to strike." His eyebrows lifted and lowered, but under questioning he conceded that present employment was high.

A moment later he went to a favorite theme among many Tampans. "Those silly cigarettes, and so many fools using them. . . . Why shouldn't a man have a real smoke?" And he puffed contentedly.

For Tampa's thousands of Latins the festivities are frequent: seasonal events, masked dances, balls for the New Year, Christmas events. Once a year the rest of the town has a carnival season to honor Gasparilla the Pirate, whom Tampa has adopted as a raffish patron saint. A Mystic Krewe of Gasparilla rides in on a vessel that simulates the supposedly blood-coated ship of José Gaspar. Though records regarding him are vague, Tampans honor José as many other Gulf Coasters fete other sea menaces who are safely dead.

Wearing eyepatches and carefully ripped garments, brandishing cutlasses, the Krewe members stage a roaring assault, "subdue" the city and hold sway for days. There are a king and a queen, music and dancing, floats that roll through the streets and much general socializing. And over it all Mr. Plant's Moorish temple lifts its minarets.

"What's the Matter with Seventy-five?"

iii

CITIES grow generally because of a location on a river channel, the arrival of a railroad or similar developments. St. Petersburg, across the bay from Tampa, was an isolated, half-hidden spot that came into its own largely as a result of the sun above it. Few places on earth have such a friendly relationship with the unclouded skies.

"The Sunshine City," St. Petersburg announces itself to the world, and underwrites the shine. One of its newspapers gives away copies whenever the sun does not come out. As long a period as a year and a half has gone by without free papers; the average is only four and a fifth papers to the year.

St. Petersburg is a place in which more sitting down goes on than any I have ever seen, including Sicily or the Riviera. Sitting is organized, with benches spotted over most of the landscape to encourage those who wish to rest or merely to regard the world around them. The city is also the New World's capital of the "senior citizens," in which more middle-aged and older people can be found during the winter than in any other known spot.

The town is what it is largely by design, a wish to draw oldsters. St. Pete, as it calls itself, was "a spot at the end of nowhere" that realized itself by exercise of native wit and adaptiveness. This is "new Florida," newer than Tampa and other neighbors. Less than seventy-five years ago it was an area of jungles and low shores, inhabited mainly by birds and an occasional Indian.

On this long peninsula beyond Tampa, Antonio Maximo started a "fish station" in the 1840s; five years later a hurricane hit and Antonio was never seen again. Another man built a house, watched hogs and cattle for stockmen, and a handful of settlers moved in and out. It took two whiskered individuals from faraway sections, connected only by chance, to make the town.

From Detroit came "General" John Constantine Williams, a man whose beard flowed superbly down half his body. Son of Detroit's first mayor, the lordly Williams visited the peninsula in the 1870s, bought 1700 acres and envisioned a city. Now, if he could only get a railroad there . . . He met another dynamic individual, Piotr Alexeitch Dementieff-Iverskoy of Russia and Florida.

Piotr Dementieff was an Imperial Guard officer and landed proprietor who became a marshal of nobility at the Russian court. He favored the liberal politics of Alexander II; when the new imperial regime turned back to autocracy he left Russia in discouragement. A wiry man with moustachios and elegant goatee (his picture gives him the appearance of a nervous bird), Dementieff went into lumber milling and built a short railroad line in the new state.

The two men talked; one enthusiasm kindled another, and they struck a deal. Let the Russian construct a line to the spot, and he would get a large interest in the land. As for name . . . Piotr Dementieff knew just the one, that of his beloved St. Petersburg. General Williams had his own preference—Detroit. They tossed a coin and the Russian won. Eventually, however, Williams erected a big hotel and made sure that the word Detroit rose over the landscape.

Dementieff (he shortened it to Peter Demens) worked furiously. For his Orange Belt railroad he had to cover more than 175 miles of swamp, rivers and quaking land. Matters progressed badly, with delays in shipment, heavy rains, yellow fever. Once several hundred unpaid Italians milled around, threatening to hang the boss; creditors seized engines and chained them to the track. Riding back and forth

St. Petersburg: wherever you look, a nice green bench

to New York, poor Demens begged for backing; going without sleep, he pleaded with friends:

> When I wrote you that I want $20,000 between the 20th and 26th, I meant I have to have it . . . a loss of time and money everywhere. I am alone—how can you expect me to go ahead? . . . Have to organize two iron forces anew, and must have all my time to do it —instead of that have to run to Orlando to reconcile the bank, lose a whole day and certainly tomorrow will be besieged again from morning till evening. . . . Cannot buy anything from the stores . . . I will have to give up. *It kills me.*

Peter Demens lived, but he could not meet the demands upon him. Losing the railroad, his spirit crushed, he left Florida and never returned. General Williams prospered, until the ever-reaching Mr. Plant of Tampa took over the enterprise. Plant is not a popular man in St. Petersburg; the townsmen say he favored his own Tampa and kept St. Pete down whenever he could.

Still, St. Petersburg would not stay down. Its assets were its many waters, its balmy winds, rare fishing and, more than anything else, the sun. About a half century ago Americans began to go South in increasing numbers for health or for vacations. St. Pete received the well-to-do, as did other Florida towns. But more and more the elderly and the middle-class groups heard about its sun and its other attractions. When the depression came the number of such callers at St. Petersburg increased swiftly, and the town saw its chance.

These settled folk spent less than those in Miami and Palm Beach, and yet if they liked a place they would talk about it and come back. The solution was clear: Make certain that they liked St. Pete. The city bent to its task and achieved an unending municipal love affair with the elderly.

"I'm here for one reason," a spry, gray-haired woman told me, her pale eyes warm with feeling. "Because I'm welcome, more than anywhere I know, including my home town. They seem to like us here, and they do for us."

By "us" she meant the hundreds on the long green benches about her. St. Pete has several thousands of the benches, taking up space along wide sidewalks in the main streets, in the parks and elsewhere.

Early in the present century Noel A. Mitchell worried because few people stopped at his out-of-the-way office; those who walked in did so mainly to rest their feet. The businessman bought several

Shuffleboard: it came ashore in Florida

benches and painted on a slogan: "Mitchell, the Sand Man. The Honest Real Estate Dealer. He Never Sleeps."

The folks came and sat and Mitchell prospered. Others did not miss the lesson, and benches appeared in many shapes, many colors. The habit of using them became a settled one; people left hotels or apartments to take places on these "outdoor divans." Cheap colors and overadvertising marred the scene, and eventually the city announced regulations. All benches had to be of a certain size and also green. A few fuming individualists pulled in their benches, but quickly reversed themselves. The benches and bench-sitters were here to stay.

From early morning until dark or later the older people go to the benches to renew acquaintances or strike up new ones; they talk about the temperature, the folks back home, what is going on in St. Pete this week. They find they have the same interests, like bridge, know the same neighbors. Some strong friendships are formed; sometimes love (or companionship, a substitute) grows.

"They met right over there, and I saw it happen," the blue-gray-marcelled Mrs. Anson told me. "I always say, when a couple meet *three* times in a row . . ." Slight dissensions may also arise. A seventy-seven-year-older, who informed me proudly of his age, asked: "See that character down the line? Well, I been sittin' here for some years. He just moseys up and takes my place one day. I say just a word or two, and he scoots. Now he knows better!"

Yet differences of opinion are few. The town makes sure that its guests are too busy to fight. Practically all of St. Petersburg has been turned into a park and amusement place for the mature. Entertainments, games, events go on steadily on land or at the water edge. This is the world's center of shuffleboard. Those who think the game confined to shipboard are behind the times. Years ago it reached the land in Florida; St. Petersburg organized it, and today more people play it here, hour after hour, than anywhere else, with a shuffleboard association and endless tournaments.

In a setting of hundred-year-old live oaks, banyans and vines, stands the Mirror Lake Shuffleboard Center, with more than a hundred courts in operation from 9 A.M. to 10:30 P.M. The organization occupies five and a half acres of St. Pete's best downtown real estate; few things are more important here than this activity. The Center has eight thousand members, and inside the buildings the incessant busyness made me feel tired.

Every noon couples join for midday dancing in a big ballroom; in the evening thousands gather for singing. Couples play bridge by the hour, and the club counts the largest duplicate bridge league known to man. I attended one of the twenty or so balls given each season, looked at the club newspaper, and went on to bowling courts, indoor and outdoor courts for "roque," a game combining croquet and billiards; club buildings for chess and checkers, rooms for lounging, rooms for table games.

There are other areas in St. Pete: Williams Park, Waterfront Park, Bartlett Park. Organizations blossom on all sides, among them the Sunshine Pleasure club that goes back to 1903. A Municipal Pier Casino is available for picnics, card parties and dances; what was once the Elks club is a favorite meeting place for the oldsters. Youngsters of forty or less, who think old age a sedentary period, will be enlightened. Among those at St. Petersburg there may be dark moods, sad driftings, and a few may sit by the chimney and mumble into their gruel, but I have never seen them. At St. Pete the folks move around, sometimes scurry, chuckle and grin. Their games are largely participating sports, not spectator ones; the old people have been busy all their lives, and they do not wish to dawdle now.

"I've got to be *doing* something all the time," I heard a coquettish seventy-year-old tell her date on the bench. His eyes gleamed like a teen-ager's. "Then let's have some sodas," he suggested, and she was on her feet before he had the words out.

Years ago the visitors began to form state and city societies, with people from each place meeting together regularly; they thrived so much that the city provided a building for their sessions. Then came organizations by trade or profession; today there are forty-five of them. There are also stamp clubs, garden clubs, grandmothers' clubs, Scandinavian clubs, clubs of Ford pensioners, a poetry league. Free public concerts have been going on for sixty-five years, and also an open forum where anything is permitted, except politics and religion. (That rule was made after some unanticipated name-calling.) Though visitors flock in by the tens of thousands, the city welcomes all of them and encourages them to register by state. As a result of this plan friends or people with the same interests quickly find a newcomer, or he finds them. At slight provocation, meetings are called to introduce people with the same backgrounds or concerns.

For me St. Pete's brightest band is the First National Three-Quarter Century Club. To belong one must prove he or she is seventy-five or older, and I know of no sprier bunch among the twenty- or twenty-five-year olds. They talk, they hoot, they have themselves a time. Their genius is Mrs. Evelyn Rittenhouse, a lively retired actress who once played with Lionel Barrymore.

"We're exclusive in this club," Mrs. Rittenhouse explains. "There was a wrangle when somebody proposed to lower the age limit to sixty or sixty-five. One woman settled it. 'I don't want people in here that aren't dry behind the ears.'" Another, told she must give evidence she had reached seventy-five, went off with bustle twitching. "This gang is too old for me, anyway," she announced.

Soon after they first met, the men club members decided one thing: they would have soft ball matches. Two teams were formed: the Kubs for those over eighty; the Kids for those over seventy-five.

"Now you're not to run, only walk the bases," Mrs. Rittenhouse cautioned.

"Yes, ma'am," they said. They walked until the third inning, when one of the eighty-year-olders hit a grounder. The crowd screamed, the batter broke into a gallop, and since then everybody has run.

There are games for the young sprouts of other groups—the Pels and Gulls, fifty and up, but the Kids and Kubs are headliners. Thousands have watched them, rooted, and the Kids and Kubs love it. Some have paunches, some look a bit pale, but they are dapper figures in their bright-colored uniforms. It will be a long time before I forget the time I first heard the Kids break into their yell: "What's the matter with seventy-five? *We're the boys who keep alive!*"

Many others are keeping alive in St. Pete. Mrs. Rittenhouse has supervised productions of "The Old Homestead," with a cast confined to eighty-five-year olds. When she tells of her work she laughs.

"These boys and girls of mine are proving it's not how old you are, but *how* you're old that counts. My twenty-five years with these people have been great ones. They've shown me that the years beyond seventy can be the most satisfying of a lifetime. As somebody said, a well-ordered life can be like climbing a tower. The view half way up is better than from the base, and it gets finer and finer as the horizon expands."

Mrs. Rittenhouse smiles. "Age can be a great emancipator. The young are bound by a thousand restrictions. They run with the herd, keep up with the Joneses. We oldsters can thumb our noses at everybody else and do what we please. Birthdays have lost their sting. We can't stop the clock and we don't give it a thought. We aren't slaving to make a living now . . . we're just living."

She frowns. "Naturally we don't like the quip along the Gulf

Coast that we're the 'city of the unburied dead.' Ridiculous! Romances are born here every hour. The winter's hunting time. While some of the game may seem out of season, the chase is fun. As they tell *me,* you're never too old to yearn." Yet Mrs. Rittenhouse does not favor some matches. "A lot of those green-bench flirtations . . . they shock me! The courtship is so—well, aggressive. Of course, when you've passed seventy-five, you may have a reason for hurrying. Still, I tell them now and then that it isn't love—just a case of somebody wanting a nurse, a provider, or a caretaker."

Nevertheless love does bloom under the swaying palms, and I watched one beaming couple at a church. He was seventy-nine, she seventy-five; the crowd included their children by former marriages and hundreds of their new St. Petersburg friends. It was a happy occasion and a moving one. Leaving the church, I noted again some of the things that the city has done for the old folks in their new home. Downtown street curbs are sloped to make for easier steps, or to help with wheelchairs. Public buildings, churches and many offices have ramps.

A limited number of the older people of St. Pete have jobs, full-time or part-time. Whether they are here on pensions or savings or if they work, most of the oldsters watch their money. For that reason, perhaps, St. Pete appears to have more cafeterias than any town its size. "If you watch yourself," a grandmother advised me, "you can get more for your dollar here than any other place I know."

You get other things, too. In arcade after arcade, you can have your blood pressure taken. Doctors and clinics flourish. If you get into trouble, financial or otherwise, St. Petersburg has a counselor to give advice and guidance. There is a city-owned and -operated solarium for sunbathing at a low fee; lip reading classes, swimming, singing and dancing classes. I saw a man of eighty-two starting to learn the Australian crawl, a woman of eighty-four singing with surprising clarity.

For the oldsters and for others St. Pete has another special attraction—baseball. An elder citizen, deep-voiced and quietly determined, made Florida the nation's spring baseball training capital. Before World War I, Albert Lang came here for his health and stayed on to become mayor. Many times he read of teams locked in because of snow. Al Lang was a baseball buff and a St. Petersburg buff, and he went to work.

Repeatedly, relentlessly, he pitched arguments, appeals at one team, then another. He offered the town's support, even when the town was not too much interested in the scheme; he spent his own money, used friendships and school ties. As other cities glared, Al Lang won the St. Louis Browns, the Boston Braves, the New York Yankees. These and other teams arrived in the spring and kept on coming; with them they brought home-town fans and followers in general. The arrangement makes everybody joyful, and St. Pete reminds you that it is Florida's baseball center.

From training camp or anywhere else, the St. Petersburg people go steadily to "Webb City," "The World's Most Unusual Drugstore." Because the spry, one-time Tennesseean, "Doc" Webb, opened in a bad location, he had to make the world go to him, and he did, with bargains, ballyhoo and "surprises." Customers arrive to see what Doc has for them today and leave with armsful, some of it deserving the name of loot.

Once "Doc" Webb offered breakfast—an egg, two pieces of bacon, three slices of toast, grits, ham gravy—for nine cents. Again he let you "buy" dollars from him at eighty-nine cents; he got you in again by buying the dollars back from you for a dollar thirty-five. As you move about Webb's, the Doc's voice may boom over the microphone. "Now hear this!" For the next thirty minutes one of his departments may sell a nationally known product for seven eighty-five, instead of the standard figure of twenty dollars. The crowd runs to the department.

Meanwhile, on a large stage, the folks may be entertained by tightrope walkers, teams of wrestlers, a man who "milks" rattle-snakes of their poison. At another time Webb offers a circus or a "water follies" at cut-rate admissions. He has a "park-a-baby service," with play pens, toys, attendants, and arrangements to page the mother if necessary. Officers in crow's nests outside direct autoists to available parking places. Another occasional service: a free ride on an elephant if you're in the mood for that.

This is even less a "drugstore" than most American places of that name. It is a store with about sixty departments, five restaurants, a supermarket, a place to cash checks at almost any hour, day or night, seven parking lots and a dancing studio. Nearly fifty thousand people a day have gone through its doors, and it has done more than twenty-eight million dollars of business a year. Its main division covers four blocks, with extra separate units such as a feed store, a service station, which also includes sporting goods and hardware; a new six-story building with furniture, carpeting, children's wear and

toys; a souvenir and information unit with data about everything in the area, including, of course, Webb's.

The Doc has "feuding" contests between departments, with clerks in hillbilly dress, competing in bargain offers. Or you may sometimes eat chili as you sit down and watch a man being shot from a cannon. It is all folksy, corny, ridiculous, highly profitable and, in a way, wonderful. When I was last there I heard a story that made Doc rise in my estimation.

Like others in St. Pete, he hires older people. One day one such man approached a day's end with drooping shoulders, in perspiring fatigue and depression.

Doc tapped him. "I've been watching you lately, and I appreciate the work you're doing. You're a real asset and I want you to know I know it."

The man beamed happily again.

Of late St. Petersburg is paying heed to other groups. When many of the older people leave at winter's end, the town offers its wide range of attractions to the young. During summer it gives to teen-agers and young married groups something of the same attention it provides for the old: moonlight rides on the water, seaside sports, deep-sea fishing, bridge tournaments and group games. Like other Gulf places, it is stressing summer, as well as winter, for holidaying.

Nevertheless, St. Pete remains at its core the city that looks to the older ones. It does what many other American towns may be doing in the future, as population changes intensify.

"You know, son," one great-grandfather said to me, nodding, "it isn't bad to be old. It has its points."

In St. Pete it has many points.

On one trip friends took me to several churches on Sunday, and I saw scenes that were rather hard to believe. The churches were thronged with so many of the older people that four and five services were being held; policemen and firemen stood at roped-off doors to guide the men and women in and out.

"It's this way every week," my friends explained.

Then they showed me their "drive-in church" on the outskirts. Within its walls several hundred people filled the pews; outside thirteen hundred to fourteen hundred automobiles had parked, with others who sat listening earnestly to the music and the sermon over the amplifier.

Soon afterward I heard again the defiant yell of the baseball Kids, which can be taken as St. Petersburg's theme:

"What's the matter with 75? *We're the boys who keep alive!*"

The Greeks

and the

Ringlings

iv

A NEAR NEIGHBOR of Tampa and St. Petersburg is Tarpon Springs, a sliver of Greece in America, a spot that claims one of the tightest concentrations of Greeks in the United States. They are there because of the sponges in the Gulf, that part-plant, part-animal growth whose skeleton is a commercial item not always easy to locate.

For years the area had men of mixed nationalities who pulled sponges from the shallow waters, using hooks at the ends of poles. Then John Corcoris, a Greek who worked for a packing company, thought of his countrymen, always experts in taking up sponges. A few came from Key West down on the same coast, then more, until the colony numbered thousands. The skilled divers went into ever-deeper waters, and today they descend regularly in grotesquely puffed rubber suits with helmets and airhose.

At Tarpon Springs the newcomers built a replica of an Aegean fishing village. There are dark-eyed, strong-faced girls with the sturdiness of Mediterranean women; trim, mustachioed young men and older ones with shiny black hair and teeth whose whiteness seems whiter against well-burned skin. The fleet—once sailing, now motored vessels, broad-beamed and bright-hued—goes out about four times a year, to be away for many days as they labor on "shares" under hard conditions. In a strange, blue-green, silent region they walk over coral gardens with balloon-like fish, tiny ones and monsters at their side, and danger present at every moment.

Once I watched a leavetaking at Tarpon Springs, an event gala and sad at the same time. Mothers, wives and sweethearts stood about, waving, smiling, weeping. "Take good care." "Come back soon." "Kiss the little one again."

The Greek Orthodox priest, his beard waving in the wind, gave a solemn blessing to each vessel and slowly they rode off, their names shining in the sunlight—*Pericles, Venus,* the titles of heroes, the titles of towns along the Greek coast.

Long before their return the families awaited them, ready for good news or bad. To the accompaniment of many cries, many greetings, the evil-smelling catch was transferred to a warehouse, graded and eventually auctioned. The Greeks are shrewd traders, and an auction may be a lively affair.

As I watched, an elder told me: "These young fellows—they find the fleet too tough a way to make a living, and the time too long to be away from their girls. They want easy jobs, like everybody else. I say we ought to send over for some that'll really work." To an outsider the boys appeared at least as hard-working as most Americans. He invited me back for January 6, Feast of the Epiphany, and the "blessing of the waters."

On that day, greatest of the year for Florida's Greeks, a stately procession went to the water, with the archbishop and clergy in highly adorned dress of gold and white and crimson. Devoutly, reverently, girls in replicas of old-time Grecian dress, and old women in plain American attire watched as a white dove was released ("It is the Holy Spirit"), and the archbishop dropped a gold cross ("That means Christ's baptism") into the water. At the second the cross struck the waves, a mass of divers leaped in, and one tight-limbed man reappeared, panting, smiling, with it. ("Ah, he will be lucky; this will be his year.") And for the rest of the day Tarpon Springs celebrated with wine and cheeses, cakes and coffee and flapping banners.

That day I learned the piquant story of the way the tranquil love-liness of Tarpon Springs drew its most celebrated citizen of the 1890s. He was the Duke of Sutherland, cousin of Queen Victoria, who left family and ancestral place to travel with the English woman he loved. Arriving on his yacht, prophetically named the *Sans Peur,* the couple were attracted to a piny elevation overlooking the water. Here the nobleman built "The Mansion," though, in the words of one of my friends, "it was nothing but a little clapboard house."

The duke and his new mate were happy, but Victoria was not. The Queen let it be known that her doors and England's were for-ever closed to him. The episode stirred mixed comment on both sides of the Atlantic, but the duke continued well content. When his wife died in the old country, he and his lady were married in the small Episcopal church at nearby Dunedin. The region still recalls him as a kindly fellow, though an untypical Floridian. When he visited in the area he went in state. As Karl Bickel notes, he left his yacht to the accompaniment of loud tootling by four bagpipers in swaying kilts!

Tarpon Springs has had the Greeks and the Duke; down the coast Sarasota has been equally intrigued by the Ringlings and their circus trappings. Before the Ringlings appeared, Sarasota's history was brief yet also well colored. In the 1880s a Scottish syndicate in the name of Sir John Gillespie acquired—without the bother of a first glimpse—fifty thousand acres of land. Surveyors blocked out five-, ten-, twenty- and forty-acre farms. It was a place that existed only on paper, but certain promoters described it as a great and booming settlement, telling families of Scots settlers that this was a land of "milk and honey," of fine fruit and vegetable farms, with grand city lots thrown in.

Sixty or sixty-five families landed to find only empty land and a freezing spell. In the words of Sarasota's first mayor, the only milk was in the cocoanuts. The Scotsmen huddled in tents, turned blue, and then most of them left. The syndicate reorganized, Sir John's son took over as manager, and the place began to grow. Whatever others thought lacking, the younger man missed his true Scots game of golf. He installed what some called the first course created in this future stronghold of the game, consisting of four holes, and a craze was born.

But above all Sarasota has come to mean circus. Over the sunny, zestful town hangs the shadow of a heavy-faced and heavy-bodied character, a lusty figure from the last American days when a man could extend himself without hindrance. John Ringling was one of eight children (only one a girl) born to a German immigrant and his Alsatian-descended wife. At sixteen he joined several of his brothers in the home town of Baraboo, Wisconsin, to form a "Classic and Comic Concert Company." Ultimately the Ringlings bought into a small circus and swiftly spread in all directions, absorbing rivals, until there was the Ringling Brothers and Barnum and Bailey Circus, the Greatest Show on Earth.

Mr. John came out on top of the heap of Ringlings, as an individual of sprawling interests, owner of mining land, grazing ground, oil wells, theatres, hotels and thousands of acres of land. He was a high liver, a man of flamboyant gestures, big deals, big deeds; the gaudy 1910s and 1920s let him splurge. At one period Mr. John was listed as one of the ten richest men in America—true, only tenth in line, but he thought it nice to be on the list. Shifting, juggling properties, he owned or controlled Madison Square Garden, with that famous tower apartment of his friend, Stanford White, who was in time to be glamorously liquidated in a family dispute.

About 1911 John Ringling called at the town of many islands and palms along Sarasota Bay. Admiring it, he shrewdly bought miles of beach; as his admiration grew, he settled for the winters in a plain frame house with the bay before it and the green Gulf beyond. He acquired islands which took his name or his stamp, connected them with the mainland, set out real estate developments and made plans for an ornate hotel, the Ritz-Carlton. The town recognized him as a quiet man in handsomely tailored suits, with a cane over his arm, and an expensive cigar in his mouth (a cigar that he did not smoke but replaced whenever it became limp), a steady blinker, outwardly impassive, inwardly tense.

"I haven't known many medieval barons," one Sarasotan told me, "but I think Mr. John would have been at home with them."

At his side was his wife Mable, born in Moons, Ohio, a "sweet woman" who always had the Garden Club in for meetings and did other things like that.

"She was as cozy as anybody on your block," a matron informed me.

More and more John and Mable went to Europe, where he collected star acts and she fell in love with the place, particularly Italy and, more particularly, Venice. Cozy or not, Mable caught a fever for the watery city which began to illuminate her existence.

If she could not remain in Venice, she would bring Venice to Florida. Mable decided on a new house, a palace in place of the little old thing in which they lived. (Mr. John made noises to indicate that the little old thing was all right with him, but went along with her wish.) One day Mable arrived at a Sarasota architect's office with an oil-cloth container from which she tumbled out pictures, pamphlets, drawings. These she valued so much that she seldom let them out of her sight.

Mable knew precisely what she had in mind. She had liked a great many places, including the doge's *palazzo,* and she wanted something of each; also she wished one façade to look something like Madison Square Garden, with a great tower like the one Stanford White had put there. Architects pointed out that such a top structure would be all too spectacular; Mr. John at last ordered it made lower on the ground of expense, and a New York architect modified the whole. The tower that emerged was merely imposing, with a lavish balcony around an open kiosk and a much-ornamented staircase turning a spiral to the top. At night its light was to serve as a beacon for many miles.

With Mable steadily at their side, the builders put up one of the most colossal of all Florida's residences—a pink stucco essay in Venetian-Gothic with a bay façade imitating the traceried loggias of the doge's residence. For the house Europe gave up tons of its treasures. From Spain the circus couple brought two boatloads of red tile. Mr. John had found a building being torn down and bought them all. Germany surrendered slabs of delicate marble, England veined marble; Venetian collectors poured out chandeliers and windows.

Some said that when Mr. John saw a European building, a bridge or a gate that he liked, he ordered it. He himself insisted that he acquired such items, or sections of them, only if he discovered something about to be destroyed.

"Anyway," a Sarasotan shrugged, "he got them. Whenever a ship arrived, we were sure it had something the Ringlings had picked up."

The Goulds and Astors, representing earlier American tycoon money, were breaking up their properties, and Mr. John bought what he could, so long as it looked sumptuous enough for him.

For two years the structure went on, until the world could peer at a finished *Ca' d'Zan.* Since not all Sarasotans understood the special dialect of Venice, Mable explained it meant the House of John. The home and grounds cost about $1,250,000; furnishings, except for paintings, another $400,000. In its solitary Baroque elegance overlooking the Gulf, it was a sight; even in a state with Moorish hotels and other architectural amazements, it made men whistle.

"Enough to make a doge bark," in the words of a native.

Facing the bay, this House of John had a forty-foot marble terrace with thirteen marble steps to the Ringlings' houseboat landing. Inside stood the great hall or inner court, two stories and a half high, with an arcaded balcony, monumental staircase, thirty rooms with paneled chambers, Hispano-Moresque pottery, Gothic religious sculptures, dozens of columns, stone chimney pieces, marble floors, much ironwork with the letter R, massive doors, carved heads of saints, brocaded walls, colored glass skylights and a coffered ceiling in Renaissance manner, but of Florida pecky cypress.

There was a "state dining room" with space for two dozen, a golden ballroom and a solarium decorated in Pompeian style, though without scenes of lustier Pompeian pleasures. Willy Pogany, the fashionable artist, was hired for one ceiling and ended by doing a second—the roof of the gaming room, showing Mable and a large-stomached Mr. John in Venetian costume among prancing figures, gondoliers, birds and animals. And gardens matched the house, with bougainvillaea, poinsettias and hibiscus against palms, great oaks and magnolias. Among them the eye caught pretty *putti,* grinning Italian cherubs.

Inside were portraits of John and Mable, executed by a society painter. For the unveiling, as Marian Murray tells it, the circus man invited Tex Rickard, Will Rogers and Florenz Ziegfeld, among others. Standing before John's likeness, Rogers made a remark that Ringling often quoted: "One thing's the matter. You've got your hand in your own pocket instead of the other fellow's."

With all the heavy elegance, the two Ringlings enjoyed themselves simply, high-spiritedly, and they gave a good time to many others, as well as themselves, in a world that had its share of drabness. There was something disarming, for instance, in Mr. John's bath, with walls of Siena marble, a tub of a solid marble block and gold-plated fixtures, and adjoining bedroom, with rosewood in the Empire style of Napoleon III—and a barber chair that might have come from Baraboo or Mable's Moons, Ohio.

To make their Sarasota retreat still more Venetian, Mable brought over a gondola and anchored it by a tiny island. Mr. John liked music, and they added a pipe organ that might have gone well in a cathedral, with player rolls like those used for a pianola. In the fragrant Florida evenings, while Mable gazed at her gondola, John sent mechanized Italian music roaring about the palm trees.

Ringling Museum:
the circus man
liked things Italian

Ringling's home: dream of Venice, like several doges' palaces combined

Mr. John's taste in boudoirs was not simple

By this time Sarasota had become a major focus of Ringling's interests, and in 1927 he made a decision to move the circus' winter quarters from Baraboo to Florida. Certain natives were taken aback at their first sight of the many-shaded, many-shaped circus folk, the men seven feet tall, ladies with waving whiskers, dwarfs in derbies. The town adjusted. Though always a band apart, the Ringling folk proved stable residents, who got into fewer scrapes than many of the home-grown citizens.

Then, too, merchants quickly realized what would occur; a civic boom, a magnificent mass of consumers and purchasers, would hit the town. They did, and Ringlingism permeated the place: Mable in the Garden Club, elephants in the back lots, tightrope artists practicing in their yards, spangled purple G-strings in the wash. Sarasota found thousands heading there for a look at the Greatest Show in practice and rehearsal, with stars in T-shirts, the big cats doing a run-through. The circus gave performances for the throngs, during which the local people stared in wonder, if they were not too busy selling trinkets and food and rooms. Eventually the town had a causeway named Ringling, a John Ringling Hotel, a Ringling shopping center, a Ringling telephone exchange.

While this went on, Mable and Mr. John became more and more eager followers of a culture circuit. They bought oils, water colors, statuary of many eras, many styles, but some saw a certain unity in their purchases. The couple were romantics, who wanted their art to have life in large chunks: stories of mythology, stories of burning love, burning massacre, surging masses. Understandably they favored the rococo and the baroque, the highly decorated Germanic and Italianate schools, in which something was always happening to somebody, and with curves and curls. An artist friend, who went with me through some of the Ringling possessions, tapped her lip: "Agonized sumptuousness."

One day Mr. John called in a friend or two; he and Mable were going to perpetuate their names with a museum, a shiny gem among museums. Ranging over Europe, he continued to acquire right, left, frontward, backward, in Berlin, Rome, Naples, Venice, of course, and other places: doorways, balustrades, pictures, whole columns of buildings. He read art books, studied manuals, lingered around galleries; he bought Tintorettos, Murillos, Rubens, Rembrandts, some cheaply, some at high rates.

In London the Duke of Westminster had been trying vainly to get rid of a famous set of four Rubens "cartoons," outsized paintings

Sunken court, statuary, *putti* in the greenery

"Circus Hall of Fame": a horse could also be ornate

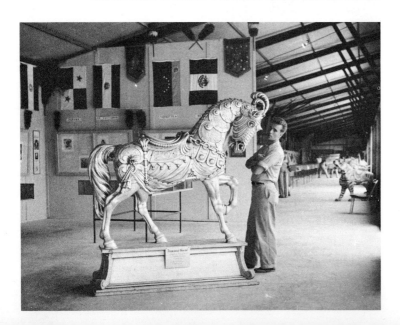

used as a basis for tapestries; they were far too big for practically anyone on earth. Ringling saw them, wanted them. An advisor urged strongly against the purchase; how would he find room for them? Ringling shook his head. He liked things big, and he'd make a place to fit them. He paid twenty thousand pounds.

Soon Mr. John had five hundred works, some mediocre, others superb. Among his holdings was the largest collection of Rubens in the United States, and paintings which made it probably the most important Baroque museum in the country. The building cost about a million and a half dollars, and the collection is worth perhaps three or four million more.

In a park near Sarasota Bay, the museum had a formal garden court surrounded on three sides by galleries lined with loggias and more than one hundred original Italian columns. Sculptured figures stood in rows above the balustrade; others of bronze and stone— athletes, kings and gods—clustered about the garden in such numbers that they seemed to be holding mass meetings. Inside were hung Rembrandt's "Descent from the Cross," an El Greco, a Titian, Van Dykes, works of Veronese, Gainsborough, Sir Joshua Reynolds, Guercino, Salvator Rosa. Eventually officials added a small eighteenth-century playhouse taken intact from Italy.

But before the museum opened, Mable Ringling died; she had enjoyed her House of John for only a few years. Ringling took a second wife, unhappily, and the marriage went to the courts. By then more troubles rained upon him. The Florida boom broke, and the market crashed. Ringling had overexpanded, overspent. His fortune was estimated at fifty million dollars, but he had little ready cash. Creditors darted forward with suits. Understandably Mr. John developed heart trouble, and sadly he watched others take over his circus.

In 1936 he died, leaving a will that further moiled affairs. In one section he made executors of his sister and his nephews, John Ringling North and Henry North; in another he disinherited them, yet accidently kept them as executors. And to Florida the circus lord proposed to leave his ornate museum and Mable's residential recreation of Venice. Factions crystallized among the descendants, and for more than ten years matters were in a furious tangle.

Then John Ringling North proved a man in the Old Master's pattern. He scored in skirmishes, he showed himself an artist in razzle-dazzle, and he won control of the circus, despite mishaps that he suffered, including the worst accident in the history of circuses—

a fire that killed 185, injured 450 and meant damage payments of four million dollars. Since then the new Mr. John has set his own imprint on the circus, reorganizing, offering glamorous gorillas and Broadway musical styles of entertainment. In recent years all circuses have suffered; North has necessarily retrenched, but the Ringling shows hold on.

John Ringling North remains a dominant figure over Sarasota. He is a man of simple tastes, mainly the best: Twenty-One in New York, Prunier's and Maxim's in Paris, vintage champagnes, work and play through all the dark hours, to bed at 7 A.M. or 8, up before dusk. He looks like a puckish Napoleon; he tap dances, plays the saxaphone and casually deals in millions.

Dark-visaged like his uncle, North has taken on much of the older one's baroque style: air-conditioned private railway car with servant quarters, imported foods and wines, large appetites and large designs for living. In the past year or two North has faced new attacks from relatives and others, and has ordered further drastic cuts, making the circus largely an indoor show rather than one under the traditional big top. But whatever happens, Sarasota expects to continue in one way or another as a circus town.

Like most who go to Sarasota, I found myself fascinated with the circus trimmings, with the retired giants who run a motel, acrobats who have their own restaurant, figures that flipped through the air as I passed a bungalow, clowns who talked at the supermarket about their grandchildren's teething problems—all the rowdy, gentle, troubled, happy world of the big top.

The state of Florida operates the John and Mable Ringling Museum of Art, the Ringling residence, and in recent years a Museum of the American Circus. For some the last may be as arresting as the first two; it is a collection of circus items, with sixteenth-century European drawings; rip-roaring "rat bills" in which competing circus men made furious charges at one another; paraphernalia used in magic tricks, and ancient parade wagons, gold and blue and yellow, juxtaposed in a kind of surrealist dream.

There is a certain surrealism, too, in the contrast of this "new" Florida and two stranded relics of an older era. About nearby Bradenton is the Manatee country, named for the gentle sea cow, the herbivorous mammal whose head has a bovine look, whose taste is of pork with a hint of fish oil. The Manatee area was settled a century and a quarter ago as a sugar region, and for twenty years or so the stalks grew tall along the water.

"Braden Castle," the people called a massive-walled residence, two-storied with four high chimneys. As late as the 1850s Indians continued a threat and the house became a fortress under attack. Only five years before the Confederate War alarms sounded, and families ran in from several directions. The red men seized slaves, livestock, and anything else that came to hand.

Steamboats rolled into the Manatee area to take away the heavy crops; the Old Southern atmosphere was strong here. Sugar cane died away with the war, to be replaced by citrus and vegetables, but "Braden Castle" survived the conflict, Reconstruction and other troubles until early in this century, when fire seared it. Now the roof is gone and the gray bulk stands alone in its wreckage, with a tourist camp about it in a strange neighborliness.

At Ellenton, a short way off, is the Gamble mansion; by contrast, few of Florida's pre-war sugar mansions stand in such preservation. Here Major Robert Gamble had three thousand acres. The building, a Greek temple in design, had a Florida touch: crushed oyster shell used in making the walls. Judah Benjamin, another planter and attorney of Louisiana, was the major's friend.

Under the Confederacy, Benjamin became Secretary of War and then Secretary of State. With the South's collapse, Jefferson Davis, Benjamin and other high officials rode down in an uncertain odyssey. Members dropped off one by one, and at last Benjamin arrived in Tampa and slipped over to the Gamble property to stay in hiding. Tipped off, Northern officers pushed in, but Benjamin jumped out a back door to hide in the woods while the enemy threshed about him.

Afterward the Confederacy's War Secretary reached a small yawl and made a perilous trip down the Gulf Coast of Florida. The vessel hid for a time at Gasparilla Island, eluded pursuers, but finally had to admit searchers. Thrusting on a cook's cap, Benjamin rubbed grease and soot on his face and succeeded in his imposture. Benjamin escaped, and went on to a second and brilliant career in England. Today the Gamble Mansion is the Judah P. Benjamin Memorial, with eighteen solid columns serenely dominating its surroundings.

From Greek spongemen to Ringlings to sugar planters . . . The coast has taken them all in turn.

Fort Myers: a celebrated parade of royal palms

Into the Sea,

by

Rail and Car

v

FROM Tampa down the Gulf Coast, then across the unpopulated, grassy-wet southern area of the peninsula to Miami goes the Tamiami Trail, named for the two cities; and here Florida drops steadily, ever more perceptibly, toward the tropics. The three hundred-mile route is a procession of varieties in land and water, people and behavior.

Venice, Charlotte Harbor, Punta Gorda, Fort Myers . . . Like a number of other Florida coastal towns, the last one has its patron figure, Thomas Edison. In the mid-1880s he arrived to perform the first of many experiments for a filament in his incandescent lamp. For a time he hoped the state's bamboo would serve. Continuing other studies, he worked to develop a dependable source of rubber in the United States, struggling over hundreds of thousands of testings of hybrid goldenrod.

For years Fort Myers was intrigued as three major American figures converged upon it—Edison, Harvey Firestone and Henry Ford. The latter celebrities had a close interest in Edison's studies, visiting often at the inventor's simple wooden house, and Ford also had a residence here. Today Floridians laugh or sigh over the story that Edison once offered to give the town a system of free lights, pioneering in such municipal electrification.

Fort Myers, the tale goes, thought over the proposition and rejected it for a combination of reasons. The town would have had to provide the poles, and they would have "cost a whole lot." And mightn't everybody get electrocuted, and wouldn't such lights keep the cows awake at night? In any case, Fort Myers values Edison's memory; the Edison home and laboratory are open to the public, which may see rare plants descended from those on which he experimented, and also the cot on which he took his famous quick naps between labors.

Beyond lies Estero, heart of "Koreshan Unity," a co-operative community fathered in 1894 by Dr. Cyrus R. Teed, a New York Stater who wore tiny spectacles, Prince Albert coat, black trousers, ruffled white tie and had unusual ideas. He received an "illumination": the earth is a hollow shell with the sun in the middle. Dr. Teed conducted tests which proved it all, he said. Starting his colony in balmy Florida, he predicted it would have ten million members, and his disciples prepared for the glad day by whacking out undergrowth for future streets.

Dr. Teed favored celibacy; by this time he was on in years. Men lived in one big building, women in another, and they even had meals separately. (Here, truly, was segregation.) Members tried to keep busy by raising fruit, vegetables and bamboo. Although he had indicated he was immortal, the doctor eventually died in 1908; the colony has continued under somewhat less rigorous conditions. . . . Near here begins the Big Cypress Swamp, a morass of wet earth from which rise the great trees. Toward their bases, trunks widen for support as roots go deep into the ground, and send up twisted "knees" whose patterns reflect in the wine-dark, shadowed waters.

About the area is the realm of a latter-day, self-made wonder, Barron G. Collier, a Memphis boy who went North and made a fortune in advertisements on street cars. Collier and associates acquired a colossal one and a quarter million acres of ground, and the Florida legislature agreed to establish "Collier County" in his name. The crashes of the 1920s hurt the enterprise, but for many miles all remains Collier.

Three views of Dr. Teed's cooperative community

Now start the Ten Thousand Islands, unending bits of sand surrounded and sometimes covered by tidal waters. Here and along the shore is the domain of the mangrove, the "stilt tree" of persistent growth which, more than anything else, builds up southern Florida. The lower peninsula is largely new-made, half-made earth; when I first beheld it from a low-flying plane, I remembered a phrase: a "watery garden," a brown-green primeval wilderness, haunting in its beauty and its isolation. Not many thousands of years ago it was largely sea, and for many miles it supports no settlements of man.

Mangrove seeds float along the coast, drop into shallow waters, and soon the odd tree lifts itself. All at once there are "aerial roots" sinking like centipedes' legs into the fertile base. They collect everything—drifting bits of sand, floating leaves, debris; they consolidate, they create fresh land. At times the crashing waves win a victory, tear the sand, dissolve it, but then the mangrove is back, and after it come other growths, orchids, grasses, the strangler fig, a host of green and pink and yellow spots against the tranquil expanse.

Like other Gulf places the islands became points of escape for many an outlaw, early and late. Before 1895 other men murmured about the area's chief bad man, "Emperor" Watson. An individual with an enormous belly and hardly less enormous red beard, Watson got into trouble in Georgia and slipped into the area near Chokoloskee. When other fugitives joined him, the "Emperor" received them on his terms, which meant complete dominance.

Frequently he gave other renegades work in his fields, then settled accounts at the season's end with a bullet in their heads. Eventually a new sheriff sailed out to take him. "Emperor" Watson took *him*, taught the fellow a lesson by putting him to work in the fields for weeks, and sent him back with a warning: "Keep the hell away."

The red-bearded "emperor" grew bolder, killed or caused the killing of all too many others. At last a band of men formed, cornered and shot him. The "emperor" left no inheritors.

Soon there appear the Everglades, the hidden region which so long mystified the people of America. The Tamiami Trail cuts into it, opening a strange and provocative world. It is, as many have said, a sea of grass about one hundred miles long, forty wide, from Lake Okeechobee to the last fringe of coast. All is flat, sinking slowly southward. Saw grass, sharp-speared, with a knifelike edge; glistening water glimpsed through the emerald spread, and the brooding silence of an earlier epoch . . . that is the Everglades.

The expanse is broken here and there by hammocks of green,

Coastal alligator:
a snout, a tail,
an armored menace

topped by palms, oaks and other trees, like islands above the waves of grass. In this area the only human beings for many years were the last of the Seminoles, Indians who never surrendered to the United States, but secretly moved in their world of gold and green and water, following trails that no white men could find. The Glades has been perhaps the last large area of the United States unmapped by the outer world. The few white parties who tried to negotiate more than its border saw members die of heat and thirst, or snake and other bites, and the survivors staggered out, gasping, to be nursed back to health.

With the mid-1920s came the feat of cutting the section of the Tamiami Trail between the town of Everglades and Miami. It was a task far more overpowering than its sponsors guessed. The saying went that it would take only "men, money and machinery." More realistic individuals called it a matter of "muck, misery and moccasins." The first workers started out with axes, knives and also rifle-bearing helpers to cope with snakes and other living enemies. Fighting the razor-sharp saw grass, mosquitoes and related perils, sinking to their necks in mud and water, the men slashed and swore and slashed on. Before long everything at their command—including rock and earth intended for a roadbed—dropped out of sight in the mushlike terrain. A decision was made to cut down to the bedrock of limestone and build on that, and millions of sticks of dynamite were exploded to blast to the bottom.

Oxen dragged heavy equipment that still slipped from view in the half earth; men died of drowning, of accidental explosions. Nevertheless the trail progressed, mile by slow mile, and today it gives a cross-section view of an area that remains in many ways a place of silent mystery. Much of it is the Everglades National Park, one of the nation's largest, created only in 1947. Along the trail, or on guided trips that may be taken out of Miami and Tavernier on Key Largo, the outsider may behold an almost incredible bird and animal life.

America knows few more fecund places, few so teeming with winged things, furred or finned ones. At the water's edge a pair of slow eyes lift, and the tip of a leathery nose; an alligator slides quietly along, leaving a light trail behind him. Others are sunning themselves —sixteen-foot reptilian creatures, all fat and leathery and somnolent, until the intruder approaches, and they disappear.

There is a sudden flapping of wings and up from a clump along a lagoon soars a white heron, "angel of the swamp," his long neck and pointed yellow bill thrust before him; then another and scores of others with wild calls. Settling in another clump, they stand as if posing serenely in this man-made refuge from other men's impulse to slaughter.

Only fifty years ago the region was a scene of ruthless destruction. Women wanted the snowy egret plumes, and South Florida provided a concentration area for the softly beautiful birds. The "best time" was the nesting period, and men went out to kill them or rip off the delicate plumage and leave them dying. The young egrets cried helplessly in the nests and starved, or were caught by buzzards that hovered about for the feast.

A native might earn twenty thousand dollars in a season or so, and many fingers itched. The Audubon Society worked steadily, often under heartbreaking conditions, to prevent extermination of the egret. Laws were passed; Audubon representatives struggled to enforce them and, in several burning incidents, were murdered for their efforts. Nevertheless the egret was saved. Today he is one of a busy, many-shaded population of birds that may startle a viewer unprepared for the sight: the ibis, the purple gallinule; the rail, waders that feed slowly, then swing lazily into the air; heavy-bodied stalkers of the water, delicate-legged searchers of insects, snake birds with their long curved necks; pink-beaked white ibis, grebes darting about platter-shaped lily pads, and sometimes the dramatic loveliness of the roseate spoonbills, red and pink and white.

There are occasional deer and bears and raccoons, and, not least, surviving clusters of the Seminoles. The Indians congregate at villages along the Tamiami Trail, with palm-roofed "chikees." They know the value of a quarter, I learned, and they like jukeboxes and soft drinks as much as the next American.

"Things not so good now," most of them, old and young, assured me. "Crazy white men hurting everything, draining the Glades, cutting down animal life, ruining the place."

Beyond question, badly planned projects have injured large areas. . . .

Despite indications to the contrary, certain of the Seminoles live in part as their ancestors did, clustering about the family cooking pots of "sofkee," their staple corn dish. They wear striped dress, silver earrings and beads in many strands around the neck. And about the Everglades go red-skinned cowboys, silent and expert.

The continent's end approaches. From Miami in a southwesterly direction extends a pendant of tropical islands, their shapes

Seminoles: the style is of another day, another life

Other Seminoles: comic books, blue jeans, a newer look

and sizes altering with the years, some gaining over the water, others losing. There are uncounted hundreds of them, largely of coral and lime rock, built up through the centuries by tiny creatures that can live only in a tepid sea—the single coral coast of the United States. These waters can be dangerous; many thousands have died when hidden reefs tore at the bottoms of their vessels.

The region of the Keys is one of ever-shifting beauty, of seas and greenery of many shadings, of great clouds and drifting flowers. When John James Audubon saw it he cried out in admiration of the wild expanse, of great pink birds such as he had met nowhere else. Others have stared in wonder at the flying fish, the iridescent creatures of many hues, tiny, exotic ones and near-monsters of the waters in which the Gulf and the Atlantic have their meeting.

On the Keys men have lived precariously through the centuries. The Spanish explorers studied the islands on their way around the peninsula; when de Soto beheld them, with their occasional trees and other growths slanted by the unending winds, he called them "The Martyrs," because they looked so much like men under torment. The Keys had scattered bands of Indians who had heard of the savagery of the whites; and so, when European vessels fell afoul of the winds or waters, the Indians waited to seize their goods and whatever survived of their men. The treasure they would use for adornment, the whites for slaughter or torture. A design was fixed; eventually this would be a coast of wreckers, who kept watch to profit by accidents and sometimes, it is said, to help them happen by false signals or other tricks.

Like the rest of Florida, the keys were first Spanish, then English and Spanish again. It was long a place of fishermen from Cuba, only a hundred miles away from the lower islands. Settlers were of many nations, many hues. So isolated, yet so close to both North and Latin America, the keys were ideal for those who dealt in contraband or carried on other shadowy enterprises. With devious channels, they enabled pirates and privateers to operate easily, darting in and out to victimize vessels of whatever kind, or nation, came into view.

By the time the United States acquired Florida in 1820, American owners were losing vast sums. To the scene it dispatched Commodore Porter with a fleet based at Key West, then and now the most southerly settlement in the nation.

A. J. and Kathryn Abbey Hanna quote an observer who had little admiration for this last island in the line: "a resort of smugglers,

New Providence Wreckers and in fact of a set of desperadoes who had paid but little regard for either law or honesty."

Commodore Porter promptly made himself highly unpopular in the Keys; by the time he left he had cleaned up the situation to a large extent. But now Key West became the center of a legally recognized profession of wreckers. A United States court gave salvage licenses, adjusted disputes and made awards; men who had previously taken salvaged cargoes to Havana and Nassau shifted to the island town. Seafaring people moved in from a dozen places, from the West Indies, Southern Europe and also New England, with many shipmasters and crews from Massachussetts and Vermont joining the Key Westers.

The island—four miles long, not quite two miles wide—prospered greatly. Salvages of liquors, satins, laces, gold and silver totaled nearly a million and a half dollars a year. Many emphasized, early and late, that they were legitimate operators, working under legal wrecking rules, and had nothing to do with the conniving elements. Merchants built warehouses, stores and other enterprises connected with wrecking work. They erected houses with lookout platforms above the roof; "miradors," the Spaniards called such walks, and the name lasted. As wrecking surged ever higher, Key West became Florida's richest city; about 1840 its small population supposedly had more wealth per capita than any in the country.

It was a polyglot settlement.

As one man said, the Key Westers, "coming from almost every country and speaking almost every variety of language, brought with them habits, manners, views and feelings . . . in many cases totally dissimilar and contradictory."

Not least was an element the island designated as "conchs," Bahaman whites who originally had migrated from London. Their accent, firmly maintained, had more than a suggestion of cockney. And Negroes, free for the most part, also arrived from the Bahamas, with a suggestion of the same speech.

The tight little island had its own name among the natives: "The Rock." Houses had no cellars; it would be difficult to dig into the hard base. They were largely of wood, the material that came most easily to hand or to salvage. Residences clustered together, big next to little, with galleries and slatted windows to admit all possible air. Cisterns stood at every turn; fresh water was precious in this tropical, salty spot.

For the wrecking gentry, however, change was on the way. The United States built one lighthouse after another. Passages became safer, and when steam navigation reached the ocean-going stage, dangers along the coasts declined. Wrecking dropped steadily away. Meanwhile Commodore Porter had urged that the island be made a major American fortification; its "advantages as a military and naval station," he thought, had "no equal except Gibraltar." Heeding the advice, the United States built the heavy Fort Taylor and further strengthened defenses in the area.

With the Confederate War a large group showed sympathy with the South, yet the town stayed in Union hands. Southern blockade runners darted about the Keys; three hundred were seized and brought here. The years after the war saw many changes, many of them good for the lively community. From revolution-torn Cuba came cigar makers to establish a major industry with a still livelier band of workers. Key Westers had a fervent role in helping finance fighters for freedom in Cuba; during the Spanish-American War the island served as a vital naval base, and for a while all the Atlantic fleet converged here. For the townfolk the goose hung higher than ever.

The Greek sponge fishermen set up their first Florida industry there, going to the nearby shallow banks to bring up thick cargoes. Every year Key West took on a richer coloration, a more zesty flavoring . . . Then troubles began. In 1886 fire broke out when the town's single steam engine was in, of all places, New York for repairs. In twelve hours flames ate half the wooden houses. Soon afterward the cigar industry started to move to Tampa, and the sponge divers went to Tarpon Springs.

With the early 1900s a pinch was being felt; sadly one family after another shifted to other towns, until a happy change was announced. Up at St. Augustine, Miami and other East Coast points, the railroad man, Henry Flagler, had spent millions and gained more millions; now the Panama Canal was to be dug, and the usually canny entrepreneur visualized the Latin South as a source of new and blooming riches. Flagler was seventy-five when he let it be known that he was going to build "the railroad that went to sea," the over-water extension of his line from Miami.

The scheme made men's mouths drop open. Flagler would push the railroad one hundred thirty miles from one key to the other, send it over swamp and morass, anchor it on land whenever he could and span the waters between. It would end at Key West, which would be his great port, connecting point of his railroad empire with the world's steamship lines. To engineers it was a fantasy; as a friend put it, "Flagler, you need a guardian." All but one contractor refused to bid; when that one would do the work only on an expensive cost-plus basis, the tycoon assigned his own forces to the task.

"Flagler's Folly" proved harder than anyone expected; its completion was a great achievement of the era. Simply to get workers and materials to the scene presented staggering problems. Most equipment had to be floated; excavators sank, ships were lost, and the Keys and their waters fought back with problems of waves and erosions at every turn. Men drowned; hurricanes washed away large sections of construction. Again and again plans had to be halted and new methods attempted. And always the unanswerable question: Would the scheme really work, or would a truly bad blow topple everything into the water?

Not least of the troubles were the workmen; at the height four thousand were needed for labor in raging heat and danger and under extreme isolation. Cubans, Negroes, occasional Scandinavians and Greeks made up part of the force, but the majority were dredged from Northern cities. Key Westers called them "tramps, bums and derelicts." Flagler didn't like to drink, and therefore he thought nobody else should. Women were few; even comic books had not yet been invented. The result was, as a Key man chuckled, "one long hell on earth."

Still the work was pushed on, almost feverishly. Flagler wanted to see his great achievement while he was on earth. It continued nearly eight years, and at last, in January of 1912, the line was ready, the first trip an international event. At Key West the eighty-two-year-old Flagler welcomed agents of foreign nations, congressmen, a governor or two. Twenty thousand Key Westers, many of whom had never set eyes on a railroad, roared a welcome. A circus came over from Havana, there was a Spanish opera and, as Sidney Martin pointed out, a thousand children threw American beauty roses at the smiling old man. By God, he had done it!

Flagler rode home and died a year later. He never knew that his sea-going line, at least for the purpose he intended, was a failure. Trade from Latin America went to other ports; though the railroad rolled back and forth for years, it "carried nothing to nowhere for nobody." And poor Key West suffered one new blow on top of another. Tariffs against Cuba injured its markets there; steamship lines dropped it, and even the Army, Navy and Coast Guard left. Population fell from twenty thousand to fifteen thousand, to twelve thou-

"Theater of the Sea": the smiling porpoise

Gulf Coast pelican: feathers, friendliness,
and a great big appetite

Key West: the old
captain's walk remains

"Oldest house on the island"; it was designed to last

sand. Rumrunning during Prohibition helped, but not a great deal. Parts of a highway were built from the mainland, with ferries to fill the gaps, yet not many people came.

When the depression struck in the 1930s Key West went bankrupt. A large part of its people asked for government relief; rubbish piled up on the streets and the town defaulted on its bonded debt, then made history by throwing itself on the mercy of Washington. As an experiment a Key West Federal Administration was formed, and the people rallied to a program to establish it as a resort place, a "Bermuda of the United States."

Key West cleaned itself up, as citizens formed volunteer bands to give so many hours a week to their community. Workmen cleared lawns and neglected beaches, reopened empty hotels. Visitors increased and found the island a place of many surprises. But 1935 gave the town and the Keys yet another hard knock, one of the worst tragedies in Gulf history.

Thousands of veterans had been sent to the Keys to do varied work; officials thought full precautions had been taken for evacuation in time of hurricane. On Saturday, September 2, a tropical disturbance was noted in the Gulf, headed apparently below the Keys. On Monday, Labor day, authorities realized it was moving on the area. Hastily the overseas train started on its way to rescue the people. There were delays and at the village of Islamorada, on Upper Matecumbe Key, confusion and terror broke among veterans and their families.

Just as the train reached the settlement a shrieking fury of rain hit it, with winds at a terrible velocity and water twelve to eighteen feet high. Every railroad car toppled over; only the engine stayed upright. Men, women and children were swept into the water or carried into groves of mangroves to drown. Some tied themselves to anchored boats in a hopeless effort to escape; others died before they understood what was happening. . . . Elsewhere lines of settlements were wiped away, mile after mile of railroad embankment washed out, the rails twisted like strands of rope.

Five hundred or more people died, and their bodies were found for days afterward, bloated in the sun or rolling with the tides. Officials ordered mass cremations; today an eighteen-foot memorial, with a scene showing palms bending ominously in the hurricane, stands at Islamorada.

The storm ended "the railroad that went to sea." Bridges and trestles came through unhurt, but other damages were enormous.

What resulted, after many conferences, was a substitute overseas highway which followed much of the route of the old line. "Flagler's Folly" had served a purpose, opening the way for an operation only slightly less remarkable. Trestles constructed for one railroad track now carry twenty feet of highway; one bridge extends for seven miles, ranking among the world's longest. To go along it is to feel much like an automobile rider speeding over the ocean.

Key West's story has had a pleasanter sequel. The world comes again to see the place and the other Keys; thousands are building homes, hotels and motels. Fishing prospers, with a shrimping fleet and the catching and canning of turtle meat. Enormous shelled creatures, captured in the outer waters, rest in the turtle "crawls," their pale flippers moving back and forth as they await their fate. And the region is, as ever, one in which sport fishing—the pursuit of silver tarpon and other game fish—draws people from many points.

Its past is reflected often in the Key West of today, with its fish docks, launches and other craft, and a flavorsome town life in the center. Under the warm sun the air is sometimes like that of Cuba, with a leisurely step and a Latin smile. Coffee shops serve small cups of the inky beverage; in the restaurants the accent is Spanish, the dishes those of Havana, with special items such as well-cooked turtle stew and pies made of the special lime that thrives here.

As I went by, a pair of elderly women exchanged remarks that might be heard around a London corner; the cockney accent of the "conchs" has yet to be lost. A moment later another bit of English speech came from a *café-au-lait* man in a bright green suit. Bahama, New England, Cuba . . . Each element has left its mark, as part of that particular Key West look—wooden houses with many porches and slatted windows to admit a maximum of air, and old captain's walks or "miradores" at the top.

The cisterns are going; in recent years the military has brought water in pipelines. Looking closely, I discovered signs of protection against blasts of wind, foundations of buildings sunk deep into the coral rock.

"Still, we don' worry about hurricanes," a fisherman shrugged. "We know how to handle ourself' when they hit. The weather people know a lot more than they once did too. And don' you hear more than ever about those murdering winds in the East and West?"

He turned to a more vital subject—buried treasure. Each key has its tale of pirates, massacres and devious doings that involve heavily encrusted trunks or sunken ships packed with gold. Now and then coins or rotted containers are found. They may not have much value, and yet each incident sends hunters racing in new searches.

My new friend had a question. "You like to go shares with me? My grandpapa, he *knew* this fellow, and the night the ol' man died he reach' for the map. This very map, mister, an' . . . ."

In another way history is repeating itself at Key West. Once more the American military are watching this area. World War II and the years that followed saw a new realization of its importance. As Henry Flagler once looked to the Panama Canal, so do officials of today, and Key West may have a large part in the building of protective rings about that artery. The Key West naval station operates, among other facilities, a sonar school and submarine base; destroyers, warships, submarines and other vessels appear and reappear in the patrolling of American shores.

The true Key Wester takes these changes, like everything else, in stride. A white-haired woman yawned and rocked as she spoke. "*Whatever* happens here, I won't be surprise'."

Sand baked by a fervent sun

Cleaning the conchs
for the Key Westers
and guest

Boat for hire: What would
you like to see, mister?

The Bragg home: style in Mobile could be imposing

No Blues
in the Night

vi

"From Natchez to Mobile . . ." So wailed the writer of "Blues in the Night." But if there are many blues in Mobile, Alabama, the city keeps them hidden. With Mobile and her bay we first meet France on the Gulf. It is this French base which, I believe, explains much about the town and her philosophy, the things that make her as different, say, from Tampa, as Tampa is different from Houston.

Mobile is the town of a quiet good time and good talk as well—the French art, modified by the Southern locale, of bright, brisk conversation. And Mobile never takes herself too seriously; she can snicker at her foibles, her characters and her own character. A one-time Mobilian, Eugene Walter, had one of his protagonists say: "Down in Mobile they're all crazy, because the Gulf Coast is the kingdom of monkeys, the land of clowns, ghosts and musicians, and Mobile is sweet lunacy's county seat. . . . You used to say you were never the same after living there, and I reckon I'm not either."

How far Mr. Walter's tongue was thrust into his cheek may be questioned; nevertheless, Mobile is a city of great talkers, of chucklesome yarns about its cousins and uncles and the people down the street. It is changing, but it retains (despite some businessmen) its avenues of majestic double files of oaks, and many of its iron-galleried buildings in a style that rises out of France, the Greek Revival and Southern climate. Sitting there, beneath an old-time ornamented punkah in place of air conditioning, I have listened gratefully as the Mobilians recalled their past.

As in Florida, the Spanish passed by first, yet they failed to stay here. They found the well-indented bay with the Mobile River and others, including the Alabama and Tombigbee, tapping many miles inland. A century and a half went by until 1699, when the French moved upon the coast. New Orleans was then only a somewhat wet stretch in an even wetter expanse up the Mississippi; the first capital became a point near modern Biloxi, Mississippi, to the west of Mobile.

The pioneer French, headed by the brothers Iberville and Bienville, happened upon Mobile Bay and explored an island near shore, on which they made a gruesome discovery. "A mountain of bones" had piled up for three or four years on the spot, a chronicler said; the heads of the men and women had been cut off. The Frenchmen called the spot Massacre Island and later changed that to Dauphin, entry place for the region.

Within a year or two the capital of Louisiana was shifted to Fort Louis de la Mobile, up the Mobile River. Affairs went poorly. Among many items which the settlement lacked was a vital one: femininity. Young men chased after Indian maidens in the woods, and officials wrote home begging for girls. The answer came in the shape of the celebrated "casket girls," *filles à la cassette,* not rich but chosen for their character and given a dowry from the king—a small trunk with neat clothing for a new life.

Being in such short supply and heavy demand, the new cargo had to be heavily guarded. During the day they could be eyed by some of the pining bachelors; at night a sentry kept guard. Most of the group were pretty, though we are told that one "looked more like a guardsman than a girl." Nevertheless, all were swiftly spoken for, including the guardsman type. Two men threatened to kill each other over her, until the commandant made them draw straws. Within a year the first baby was born, and so many families claimed descent from the maidens of the caskets that they have been pictured as the most fertile misses who reached the New World.

Classic revival in Alabama: Government Street Presbyterian Church

Not long afterward, in 1710, the Mobile River site flooded and the fort and capital of Louisiana were shifted to the present site of Mobile. The streets took names that have never been lost: Conti, Royal, Dauphin. But there was disappointment when the capital eventually moved to New Orleans. With some effort Mobile clung on, and to this period dates the story that Mobilians tell and retell of another "Anastasia" of Russia.

An early settler was a young blond woman, beautiful, sad-faced. Saying nothing about herself, she took a small house. Clearly she did not need funds, for she dressed handsomely and wore fine gems. She obviously was an aristocrat with a tragedy behind her. A certain Chevalier d'Aubant was drawn to the pensive lady, and after a time she told her story to him.

Some years earlier Alexis, the gross and twisted son of Peter the Great, had appeared in one of the German duchies to ask for the duke's daughter, Charlotte, in marriage. To have one of the family as a future Czarina! Charlotte's father was delighted. She had no choice; she was bitterly unhappy as Grand Duchess Charlotte in St. Petersburg, and finally she ran away. Not daring to return to her family, she went to Paris and joined a party for Louisiana.

As he listened, the chevalier remembered that he had gone to the Russian Imperial Palace once or twice. Now he knew why the handsome face had been so puzzlingly familiar. Yet he and others recalled accounts of Charlotte's death. She explained: To hide the facts, a false tale had been invented. By now d'Aubant had fallen in love with the gentlewoman; they married, and when he went back to Paris she accompanied him.

There his circle accepted her and she won their approval in everything. The chevalier died and the widow lived on as before, until one day she discovered herself before the wrong person. He had known the Grand Duchess Charlotte, he exclaimed, and this was not she, but a woman from the same German duchy who had been only an attendant! They looked alike; the pretender had managed to take some of the dead Charlotte's jewels and costumes and slip out. . . . The false Charlotte retreated from view and died later in sad straits.

As the Mobilians say: "She should have stayed right here. It's better to be satisfied with a little than to reach out for too much."

From the dense forests about the bay Mobilians built early houses on raised pilings to keep floors dry in rain or flood. For a long time life was far from easy, but the settlers showed a Gallic gaiety that helped them survive highwater, hell from the Gulf and other problems. In August of 1704 Governor Bienville had proclaimed a holiday for a bright Masque of St. Louis. Seven years later the Mobilians had a New Year's Carnival of Boeuf Gras, or Fat Beef.

"Those were the times," say the Mobilians," when we first got our Mardi Gras in our blood, and we've never let it leave us."

Under the French, Mobile received something, little noticed at the time, which would later be well remembered—an oriental flower, previously transplanted to France, called the azalea. But a few years later, by the 1760s, the Mobilians had more than white-and-pink flowers to concern them. The French mother had to give them up, and England was on its way to the Gulf.

The Mobilians blinked through their tears as the fleur de lis dropped, and the British flag rose in its place to the accompaniment of music by Highland bagpipers. Many, as true Frenchmen, left; others, more realistic, stayed and the town remained largely Gallic. Nevertheless, Fort Condé became Fort Charlotte after England's Queen, and new names were displayed: Stuart, Mather, McIntosh. England had great hopes for Mobile; one commentator noted that its bay could "contain the whole British Navy." Mobile might be a future back door through which to reach for valuable New Orleans. But over in New Orleans that city's Spanish masters had *their* minds on Mobile. During the American Revolution, Galvez of Louisiana marched upon both Mobile and Pensacola, and after seventeen years England followed France out of the town. Spain stayed thirty-three years. Mobile retained part of its French population, part of its Englishmen; both elements learned Spanish words for trade, practiced getting along with the new rules and kept right on being themselves, Gulf Coast folk to the core. . . . Another influence pressed upon the Mobile area, that of the Americans who pushed south and talked of their right to the fine bay. During the war of 1812 the newcomers marched in, took Mobile, and that was that.

When the state of Alabama was formed, its Gulf shore became a small stretch cut from the Florida panhandle, with Mobile dominating it. Mobile was Alabama's way to the sea and a place far more cosmopolitan than the interior. By mid-century, for instance, it had about sixty-five per cent of all foreigners in the state, and has continued as an exotic in the eyes of the inlanders—all too "different," all too highly flavored.

Most Mobilians found the change to the United States a rewarding one. Thousands of river acres opened up above the bay. Cotton was spreading over the South, and Mobile was now a cotton town, with additional Negroes and mulattoes. Steamboats made a thickening line on the Alabama streams, and along their banks growers built their versions of classic establishments. By the 1850s only New Orleans stood ahead of Mobile among the world's cotton ports.

In the words of one observer, Mobile was a place where "the people live in cotton houses and ride in cotton carriages. They buy cotton, sell cotton, think cotton, eat cotton, drink cotton and dream cotton. They marry cotton wives and unto them are born cotton children." With all that there blossomed a Mobile style in building. Some were small "Creole cottages," with brick between wood and a simple European pattern; others, more imposing, appeared with high-ceilinged rooms. They showed the influence of the Greek Revival on the exterior, but also touches of both France and Spain.

Nearly always there were balconies—not around all the house or on three sides, as in the rural sections, but taking up only the front or part of it, with slim columns in a restrained design. Fine doorways, fanlights and simple steps became the marks of the new style, and as a final detail, ironwork railings, wrought or cast in imaginative, richly ornamented fashion. A number of iron galleries were two-storied, almost monumental, and here and there they extended over the entire sidewalk to provide a shaded passage for Mobilians.

Such establishments lined Government Street, the city's most important thoroughfare. When Mobilians set up a double line of master oaks along it, Government Street was on its way to rank as one of the great thoroughfares of the South. Meanwhile there was another reason for the continued French touches about Mobile. Toward the city, soon after Napoleon's fall, there headed a band of followers of the Corsican, who had chosen to test their fortunes in the New World.

Romantically the newcomers named themselves the "Association of French Emigrants for the Cultivation of the Vine and Olive." As members of that organization they received congressional land grants on the Tombigbee River beyond Mobile, and now the barons, counts and colonels arrived to try a region that had once belonged to their common mother, France. At Demopolis, "City of the People," and Aigleville, "Town of the Eagle," they erected log cabins to house their rich carpets and chandeliers and started to farm among Indians, frontiersmen and uncomprehending land squatters. None of them

Admiral Semmes house: the special Mobile manner, with ironwork

had ever held a plow; they were accustomed not to the country air, but to the drawing room and the minuet. They failed in one venture after another. As Caldwell Delaney declared, a colonel eventually ran a small ferry while his marchioness-wife cooked flapjacks at the riverside for the customers. A number returned to France, a few to New Orleans, while others settled in Mobile and Springhill outside the town. Various exiles then succeeded in urban pursuits, giving a new gloss to the city's affairs.

By the 1840s Mobile had ranked as one of the major centers of Southern society, a place of the theater, horse racing, shopping by planters' wives at establishments that offered Irish laces, Parisian dresses, Italian ornaments. Charlotte Cushman, Lola Montez, Edward Forrest, Joe Jefferson, Tyrone Power, Junius Brutus Booth . . . Mobile saw them in turn.

The town was becoming increasingly a place of the Mardi Gras style of celebration. On New Years' Eve of 1830, as the story goes, a roistering evening by a bright party of men led to formation of Mobile's first "mystic" organization. After visiting a series of bars, the party pounced on several rakes and cowbells on display before a store. "Shall we?" They did. Seizing the implements, they went forth to wake all Mobile and apparently succeeded. Greeting them with blinking eyes, the mayor asked them in for a drink, and the Cowbellion de Rakin Society was conceived.

Thereafter the affair was an annual one, with a secret membership, masking, and in time parades with large floats that rolled through the streets with the classics or legends as flamboyant themes. Firecrackers popped, rockets shot across the skies, bands played, country people from the outlying areas beamed and Spanish cake sellers moved about the crowd. Members of the mystic organization kept their identities secret during the parade and later, at a ball with tableaux, symbolic scenes of pageantry and dancing. At the end the men, still masked, would march away into the night. Additional organizations formed, names changed, but the design was fixed.

This social picture was, of course, not the whole of Mobile. The heavily crowded waterfront had its own pleasures: garish bars patronized by men of the sailing vessels or hard-handed, hard-tempered boatmen from up the rivers. Roaring fights would break out; lights would be shot away and a body or two left in the alley. There were gambling places in which richly dressed, shrewd-eyed "fellow passengers" fleeced cotton growers on their arrival in town, and shining establishments for gentlemen, which promised that all tastes could be gratified. For Mobile was a Gulf town, and a tough, hard-living place.

Meanwhile at the other end of the city, in the more rarified air, Mobile had its Great Lady, Madame LeVert, hostess, friend of the celebrated and a wit, though sometimes too sharp a one. The blond Octavia was daughter of a former governor; she learned six languages, stirred admirers in her early teens and went to Europe, where Queen Victoria reportedly paid her highly unusual notice. Elizabeth Barrett Browning, Lamartine and the Empress Eugénie were also taken by her. Marrying Dr. LeVert of a well-placed French family, Octavia then set up what was, by all accounts, a remarkable salon.

To her receptions went the glittering stranger to Mobile, the Bohemian, the novelty on the social scene, the old guard in "a social jambalaya not possible to match in all Dixie." Madame LeVert threw everybody together, as she had seen such things done on the continent, and enjoyed the result. Some women detested her, while others giggled at her strivings. Yet, as Mr. Delaney has commented, she was also a generous woman. When Joe Jefferson's father died of yellow fever, while appearing in Mobile, she saved the family from hunger, and the actor-son later said: "Nothing was too high for her understanding or too lowly for her kind consideration."

For decades she was everything to Mobile, but almost overnight she dramatically dropped from grace. "You see," an older Mobilian explained in a hushed voice, "Madame entertained Yankees during the war."

With the 1860s the Yanks were on their way to Mobile. For most of the war the port served as a major Gulf center for blockade-running; with the fall of New Orleans, its importance grew still larger. From the bay hundreds of Confederate ships darted out on runs for badly needed medical supplies, war materials and also stylish luxuries for which some would pay high. Years earlier the Federal Government had constructed the magnificent Fort Morgan on Mobile Point and Fort Gaines at the edge of Dauphin Island, dominating the bay. At the war's start the Confederates promptly took them over, and General Joseph E. Johnston described Mobile as the South's best fortified town.

But in 1864 a Union election approached with strong rumblings from peace party advocates. An order went out: Take Mobile, if only to lift northern morale. From Jefferson Davis the Confederates received their own message: "Mobile must be held." Each side prepared for one of the war's raging naval clashes. Over in New Orleans

Admiral David G. Farragut, a Southerner loyal to the Union, moved out with his flagship, the *Hartford* and seventeen or eighteen other big vessels. The Confederates had a new monster ironclad, the *Tennessee,* and several gunboats. Working furiously, the Southerners had strewn the channel to the bay with "torpedoes" or mines.

On August 5, 1864, the cathedral bells burst a warning over Mobile and smoke poured forth as two hundred or more guns blasted in the distance. The Yankees were trying to run the gantlet between the forts. The heaviest federal ships, lashed in pairs, led the Union file. The Southern-held forts hit their targets again and again; masts cracked apart, riggings collapsed. Nevertheless, Farragut's forces shoved on with the admiral himself high in the rigging to see over the smoke if he could. (He was not lashed to the mast, as some say; that, Mobilians remind you, was Ulysses, a Farragut of an earlier day.)

Just beyond Farragut the Union monitor *Tecumseh* churned toward the rebels' ironclad *Tennessee* and shook with a terrible blast. She had struck one of the torpedoes and blown apart. The Union file broke in panic, and with that Farragut made his celebrated remark: "Damn the torpedoes! Four bells. Captain Drayton, full speed ahead. . . ."

The Northern forces rallied, and it *was* full speed ahead. Through the galling fire the two sides exchanged blasts. The Confederate's powerful *Tennessee* struck repeatedly at the other vessels; escaping her, they belched their fire. One Southern gunboat sank, another was caught, one got away. The *Tennessee* slipped to shelter for repairs and then amazingly ran out for a last desperate effort to ram the whole Federal fleet if it could!

The flagship evaded her; the Unionists maneuvered, thrust, and the *Tennessee* was downed at last, her smoke stack blasted away, steering equipment wrecked, port shutters jammed. Admiral Buchanan, ranking Confederate Navy officer, and many of his men were badly wounded. Farragut sent Buchanan and the others to Pensacola by ship under a flag of truce. It may also be noted that in this war of the brothers, the few Union men who did not die when the *Tecumseh* blew up were rescued by a small boat that boldly ran up a Union flag, and the Southerners declined to fire on them.

Naval history had been made. The forts had fallen and the Union had put a stopper in Mobile Bay. Yet the bay was not Mobile itself, and the town clung on, stubbornly rebel, until just before the war's close. On April 9, 1865, a garrison at nearby Blakeley gave way after a long siege. That was some hours after Lee surrendered at Appomattox. "So," comments a Confederate descendant, "we can tell people we held out longer than Lee." With the issue settled, the two commanders behaved in right knightly fashion. Bands played "Dixie" and "Hail Columbia" in friendly succession and the generals toasted each other in champagne. As a Mobilian might say: "That's Mobile for you."

The city knew bleak days, as the cotton trade was slow to revive. A visitor of the 1870s found Mobile "tranquil and free from commercial bustle . . . still as one of those ancient fishing vessels on the Massachusetts coast when the fishermen are away." In the slack years the town gave heed to another war figure, Father Abram Ryan, its "poet-priest." He had served as a Southern chaplain and sometimes as a soldier in the ranks. The son of an Irish couple, a man with pale blue eyes, leonine yellow head and locks that hung uncombed to his shoulders, Father Ryan was an individual of high emotions, frequently stirred. Almost always he wrote of pitiful, tragic themes; restlessly he moved about the country, demonstrating his gift for swaying an audience with a gesture. To this day Mobilians recite part of his requiem to the Confederacy:

> Furl that banner, softly, slowly,
> Treat it gently—it is holy—
> For it droops above the dead.
> Touch it not—unfold it never,
> Let it droop there, furled forever,
> For its people's hopes are dead.

The city has a small park, banked with azaleas, and a statue honoring Father Ryan. Mobilians point out that its outstretched hand is ever shiny, because everybody likes to touch it. And a short distance away Mobile recalls with a plaque the former home of the boy who did amateur theatricals here and rose to American immortality, Madame LeVert's grateful friend, Joe Jefferson, the actor.

That is another of the unusual things about this town. Unlike most American ones, it pays tribute to its artists, its men who were not bankers or generals. When I first came upon the memorials to Jefferson and Father Ryan, I remembered a morning in Paris when I found a gentle monument with a single name: Musset, and the French village with a tablet to a transcendant chef. (Though Mobile has some good cooks, I have yet to meet with a memorial to one of them.)

In the poet-priest's day the city had a still greater celebrity, Mrs. Augusta Evans Wilson, a mousy little woman who "talked like a book" and wrote a parade of novels of astonishing popularity— *St. Elmo, Vashti, At the Mercy of Tiberius.* She was the "first Southern writer to earn a hundred thousand dollars" and properly a town marvel. Mrs. Wilson had a white fixation, and would have only pale flowers in her garden, white chickens, cows and horses. Some had not been kind to her when she was unknown; succeeding Madame LeVert as Great Lady, she showed some of the qualities of a martinet. When she lived on Government Street and rested on the fine gallery of her house, people said:

> Miss Augusta sits on high
> And judges mortals passing by.

Mobile itself was beginning to "sit on high" again. The port, which had been neglected, was dredged; energetic men discovered a successor to cotton in the great supplies of timber around them, and simultaneously Mobile gave more heed to the Latin countries. Shippers clustered about the bay, and ultimately the Waterman Steamship company could claim rank as the biggest in the world. Industry mushroomed along the water, and today there is a steady scurry, though muted to fit the tempo of the town.

Strangers also notice a pleasant optimism among those who walk in the moist air of the waterfront, with its gray, ocean-going ships lifting decks above the wharves, and a stir after dark. Still there is the earlier, leisured rhythm on the streets, a habit of lingering over the coffee cups, time for fishing trips. Along Government Street the outstretched arms of the oaks meet high overhead, giving the serenity of another generation. The galleried houses continue, their façades shining in the sun as they did a hundred years ago, and Bienville Square remains in the center of the business area, its own oaks masterworks of Nature.

As ever, too, there is that Mobile talk. Talk about the crazy thing somebody said of the Bankhead Tunnel which cuts under Mobile's river; about certain officials who tear down Government Street oaks after dark; about the mural of the Battle of Mobile Bay at Point Clear's Grand Hotel over the water. There the artist labored earnestly over the placement of forts, ironclads and small boats. The owner was delighted with the colors, the vigor of conception, the whole thing, except for one detail. It showed the North winning.

"But the North did win," the artist observed, irrelevantly.

The outcome can be guessed; in this version the Stars and Bars carry the day.

And the talk is also, very often, of the Mardi Gras. With the war's end the festivities expanded swiftly. January 1 gave way to Shrove Tuesday, the date that New Orleans had been using, and events spread over many days. More mystic organizations, more parades, more traditions that last, little changed, into the present day: King Felix, lord of the festivities; a royal vessel; grand marches; call-outs for the dancing . . . The old Strikers organization observes that it is exceeded in American age only by the Ancient and Honorable Artillery Company of Boston and the Saint Cecilia Society of Charleston.

After one Mardi Gras visit, I went to a cemetery—not so peculiar a progression as it may seem. There friends showed me two graves with tombstones ornamented by designs of rakes and cowbells. No one in Mobile would consider that odd.

"These symbols of Mardi Gras are things we're all proud of, like membership in the Legion of Honor," one native said. In no other city, perhaps, would "Father was a Dragon" be accepted as a simple statement of justifiable pride.

Not long after Mardi Gras comes Mobile's annual azalea festival. The flower thrives here in a peculiar richness, and an azalea trail covers thirty-five miles of beautiful growth. Some trees are more than a hundred years old and thirty feet high, and they shade from white to purple with variations between. Many gardens are also open, among them the unparalleled Bellingrath Garden outside Mobile.

It was only a fishing camp when Walter Bellingrath visited it back in 1916. Son of a German immigrant and a Scots-Irish Southern woman, "Mr. Bell" was a public school graduate who made good, partly through a little-known drink named Coca-Cola. Like the Ringlings, he and his wife, "Miss Bessie," went to Europe and admired what they saw. Coming back, they achieved what may be the South's most handsome gardens.

At first the grounds of the hunting lodge received only the over-flow from "Mr. Bell's" town gardens. Then the couple noticed the effect of delicate azaleas under mossy oaks, the glossy-leafed magnolias and cedars and tall pines. This open area provided a setting such as they had not visualized. Over a sixty-acre property they placed camellias, hydrangeas, wisterias and other growths. Friends talked; people wanted to look at the gardens, and eventually more than two hundred thousand came in a year. So far, more than a million have gone there.

The Bellingraths had no children, and when they died his will left the gardens and most of his estate to a foundation to help a group of churches and colleges, among them a Negro one at Tuscaloosa. To wander about the plantings is to know a beauty which parallels, in informal fashion, that of the celebrated gardens of southern Europe. There are fountains, wide carpets of red and yellow and white flowers, open lawns giving vistas toward the water, groves of trees dominated by overpowering oaks. Through the year varying flowers bloom. With October the camellia japonicas open, twenty-five hundred of them. By February the azaleas are in warm competition, and the droppings of their thousands of blooms, white and pink and purple and crimson, hide the grass. Within a month or two mountain laurel, dogwood and white spirea bring more delicate shadings, and then the blue and lavender of hydrangeas, the flush of crepe myrtle, the quick blossoming of hibiscus and, not least, the pervasive fragrance of the sweet olive . . .

Meanwhile there is Mobile itself. I never leave without a story; from my last visit I remember two. One is about a settled lawyer who, driving over a long, hot stretch, recognized an aging Negro woman. Stopping, he offered her a ride. At the end she bowed. "I thanks you a whole lot, Mr. Will."

"Don't mention it, Lila."

"No, sir, I won't mention it."

This, of course, has a pathetic undertone; the other has none. Some time back a group of Mobilians held ceremonies honoring the famous poet-priest. A little *grande dame* told friends she had known Father Ryan real well, and repeated things he had done, things he had said. Invited to the ceremonies, the little *grande dame* sat up proudly. The speaker got up and made the statement that "only the most truly ancient Mobilians, a last few" would recall Father Ryan. At that the little *grande dame* stiffened and whispered to her neighbor: "It must have been his son I knew."

That, too, is Mobile for you.

Bienville Square: Now it was like this . . .

Egyptian, not Greek revival: lady-guards before Scottish Rite Cathedral

Ship chandler's shop:
What you want?
We got it

Mobile's Barton Academy:
stately columns above and below

On Alabama shores: a gift of the Gulf waters

A circle in crabs:
claws ready for
your fingers

"Hot Shot Furnace" and Coast Guard Light:
here roared the Battle of Mobile Bay

Mississippi coastal oak: a hill of branches and Spanish moss

Old South
on the Gulf

vii

"THE COAST . . ." From my boyhood in New Orleans, the words meant a special place, a magic area. For more than a hundred years the Creole city, together with much of the rest of the South, thought of the Gulf area of Mississippi State as its region of summer play, its holiday land, when the interior air became all too steaming and they needed a breeze-touched retreat that was not too far away.

More than any area along the Gulf, this is the Old South. For many miles there appears a procession of replicas of the plantation residences, some massive, others a warm-season version in half scale. The houses generally stand on high ridges, their brick or wooden bases lifting them still higher in the breezes. They are half hidden in their settings of downsweeping oaks and pecans and their hedges and bushes of camellias, many as big as most trees of other sections.

Yet this is that earlier South with a difference, without party clothes, taking time off to do little but rock and rest itself. In the old days men came in family groups with wives, children, horses and servants, if only to escape the harmful "miasmas" or "exhalations of the earth" that supposedly brought yellow fever and other epidemics. Although this motive is gone today, the pleasant custom goes on. Hundreds regularly rent a house for two or three months, while Father joins them for shorter periods or commutes daily to New Orleans. And some like the coast so much that they have settled there permanently.

Along the shore is an unbroken stretch of about eighty miles, always in sight of the slow waves to one side and the sentinels of trees to the other. It has no single great settlement, but a string of them: Biloxi, Gulfport, Pass Christian, Bay St. Louis, Waveland, Ocean Springs, and others with names like poems in the wind; sometimes the towns run together in a long line. For nearly thirty miles a man-made beach of white sand dazzles the eye, and over it long wooden walks extend to pavilions and boathouses with steps into the deeper Gulf.

Here flourishes another Mississippi, so different from the rest of the state that it might be of another region, more liberal in outlook, more tolerant of man's lapses. It may or may not be true, for instance, that "Mississippi will vote dry as long as it can stagger to the polls." The fact remains that in many rural and town sections a man who is rigidly against rum for the record may tipple behind the barn. He can stand up firmly to be counted against gambling, but not object to a little chance-taking when the neighbors are not looking.

On the coast, for the most part, there are no barns to hide behind, and the people next door will hardly peep at a game because they themselves may be trying their luck at the moment. These Gulf folk turn an amiable smile toward life; they think it not unreasonable for human beings to be—well, human. Much of their philosophy is explained by the fact that, along with the traditional South, there exists a pungently French life with other South European touches: Italian, Dalmatian, Greek, Spanish.

These earlier people of the Mississippi Gulf have lived to and by the sea. They are more at home in a skiff than a wagon; from the waters around them they have drawn sustenance and a certain joy and kinship with the elements. And the locale has nurtured a cuisine which for me, at least, may be the best along the entire Gulf. Here is some of the most resourcefully prepared, most imaginatively seasoned food this side of France. Though basically French, as are many things here, it has subtle modifications: new sea-things, new combinations, a bit of spice from the Mediterranean, a tingling suggestion of a Spanish herb.

The many elements get along here; over all the area, most people and things fit themselves to one another. The natives can grow excitable, shout in anger or happiness; quickly the emotions subside and a grin changes a swarthy, sunburned face. "Ah, mister, you 'ave made me mad for a secon'! . . ." A number of my friends have gone to the coast and been repelled by the ways; then they too have learned to accept life as they found it. Acceptance—that is, above all, the by-word.

Off the shore lies an irregular line of low islands, many with heavy growths, part of the continental shelf. These islands gave the area its first brush with history. Back in 1699 the brothers Iberville and Bienville landed at Ship Island, a long sand bar off the green sheltered waters of Mississippi Sound, and selected the nearby peninsula for their settlement at old Biloxi, or Ocean Springs. And today the Biloxians remind you that this was the first capital, before New Orleans and even Mobile, of all that Louisiana area as high up as the present Yellowstone Park on one side and Pittsburg on the other.

For years Biloxi was the French pioneers' base and port of entry. Along the coast ships dumped thousands of bedraggled men and women, brought when John Law's Mississippi Bubble floated over France. Many died on the burning sands; the rest moved or lived on as best they could. After a time the capital was shifted to New Orleans.

"I don' know why they went and did a thing like that," a Biloxian said with a frown.

During the decades that followed, Biloxi and other Gulf settlements lingered on, forgotten or at least ignored by the great ones up the river. At remote Ship Island, in 1757, a sadistic commandant mistreated French and Swiss soldiers—maiming them, tying them naked to trees at the mercy of sun and insects—until they rebelled and killed him. France responded with a public show: one man lashed to a wheel, which was twisted until he was torn apart; others nailed alive inside coffins which executioners, using crosscut saws, cut in half. . . .

Fishermen, hunters and small growers clustered about the Gulf; ships stopped occasionally, and also pirates. One stretch of the coast, between the present Pass Christian and Long Beach, has long been untouched by man. "Pitcher's Point," the coast people call it, and they know precisely why it is barren. One of the eighteenth century pirates got mad and put a black curse on it.

"So, monsieur," a Gulf Coaster inquires, "how *kin* anything make out good there?"

Spain came to Louisiana, but the government at New Orleans made little difference to these outlying folk; they accepted a few Spanish newcomers, with Germans, French-Canadians and "Frenchmen from France," as the region terms them, and also Acadians, members of the tragic French band exiled from Nova Scotia in a clash with the English. When America took Louisiana, the governor's representative went to the coast and found "a primitive people of mixed origin, retaining the gaiety and politeness of the French, mixed with the abstemiousness and indolence of the Indian. They desire only to be let alone in their tranquility."

Some wanted to be let alone for reasons of their own. Still standing at Waveland is an impressive house dating (at least in part) to the early 1800s, with stuccoed walls, a line of columns and dormer windows offering a view of the sea. Coast dwellers have named it "the Pirate's House" and say it once had a tunnel under the road to the water's edge. Their conversation is heavy with murmurs of buried gold.

"My *grandpère*, he once have a map, or jus' part of it. When my bum cousin from Jackson, Mississippi, dies, I gonna root in his attic and get that map. Then, man, I *tell* you . . ."

His neighbor pointed toward a friend. "And that lady yonder, she know *somethin'*. Ever' now and then you fin' her boys diggin', diggin'. When you comes near and axes a question, they make like they fishin'. Someday they gon' laugh at us all and ride off in diamon' to New York."

In the speaker's eye there was only admiration. Who would begrudge a friend his hard-dug treasure? And now, as then, many show an unhidden affection for those who get in trouble with the government.

"He's a real man, a fine mean one," one Yugoslav-Acadian informed me. "It took four Federal men to git 'im, and when they hol' 'im down, what he do? He kick ten teets from dey mout's!"

Several times the outside world impinged on the coast people. Late in 1814 Jean Cuevas of Cat Island stared at a strange sight— a ponderous British expeditionary force of fifty men of war, schooners, sloops and other vessels bearing twenty thousand soldiers on the way to meet Andrew Jackson below New Orleans. The English tied up temporarily at Ship Island and a pair of soldiers went out to forage with, oddly, an Oriental cook. Jean found them killing his cattle and shot two; one nicked him in the leg. Taking Jean aboard one of their vessels, they insisted he guide them through the lakes and bayous to

A sound of countless wings: flight near Mississippi Sound

New Orleans. Jean, who knew almost nothing of the peculiar new America which ruled him, nevertheless shook his head. He would not, and he did not.

Soon afterward the waters near Bay St. Louis were the scene of a daring effort by American forces to cope with the overpowering British naval flotilla. They did not have a chance; all their five boats were sunk or caught. But they had delayed the enemy for precious hours, and the coast had witnessed the final American battle with a foreign force, at least to date, in the nation's waters.

Before long the coast gave a better welcome to other newcomers: cotton planters from Natchez, sugar growers and sugar merchants from the New Orleans area. With their families they sailed about the shining waters, rode over the new roads, topped with crushed shells from the Gulf, and otherwise enjoyed the pastoral scene. The natives watched in curiosity as the newcomers' wide-skirted daughters swung about the parlors and over the wide galleries of the big houses. Biloxi, Bay St. Louis, Pass Christian . . . Each had its followers, but "the Pass" came first. The name of this old-time social center was always pronounced "Pass Chris-chi-*an*." Here in 1849 the people of "the front" (the natives generally lived at "the back," away from the beach) formed the first yacht club in the South, and one pillared house after another went up in settings of roses and oleanders and trumpet vines.

Eliza Ripley remembered nostalgically a hotel at "the Pass" in the 1840s. The girls went regularly to the wooden piers over the water in full muslin frocks. ("Bathing suits were hideous, unsightly garments, high neck, long sleeves, long skirts, intended for water only!") The misses reappeared under parasols and veils; décolletage was unthought of, unknown. Still, "there was no lack of beaux who came, more than enough to 'go round,' by the Saturday boats, in time for the weekly hop—danced all Saturday night and returned to the weekly drudge (as they called it) in the city. The bonbons and flowers they brought vanished and faded long before the little boat with its freight of waving hats and handkerchiefs faded in the twilight . . ." Four marriages developed in one season, signalizing "the superior advantages of a hotel veranda."

About 1880 Northerners learned of the Mississippi coast and came to it in late fall when the Southerners had left. Chicagoans tended to center in one town, Detroiters in another, and the coast people were happy to act as guides and helpers.

"South'ner' in summer, Yankee' in winter—tha's a nice way," a mustachioed beneficiary said in summary.

Southern planter style, transplanted to the beach front

As Pass Christian represents the past, Biloxi epitomizes the present. It rests contentedly on three things—fish, visitors and a general taste for a good, relaxed time. It might be hard to say which means most to the Biloxian. Set on a thin peninsula between Mississippi Sound and its Back Bay, Biloxi is bordered by practically anything that can be named with fin or shell: trout, bass, sheepshead in the bay; crabs and mullet in shallows at the shore; fighting tarpon, dolphin, Spanish mackerel and kingfish in the deeper waters. Beyond wait the water crops which have enabled Biloxi to call itself "the nation's seafood basket," and the world's biggest center for canning of shrimp and oysters.

From its early years Biloxi sent out men to reap the water. Biloxi schooners have a celebrity of their own, and I have met third-generation boatbuilders.

"I grew up with shavings in my ears," a man in his seventies exclaimed, "and my boy, he the same."

He worked in a half-open shed along the bay back of his house; when not at this occupation, he joined the fleet that combs the Gulf waves.

My friend's accent was French, but several near him had the speech of the Adriatic. Fifty years or so ago the area drew men of the Dalmatian ports, Austro-Italians, and then also a few Poles and Czechs. The first few years were difficult, even for families accustomed to a hard life. Like other immigrants, they crowded in bleak, heatless shacks "and got shove' aroun' like cattles." Today my elderly friend and his grandchildren live among neighbors on the bay in plain, clean houses with an atmosphere of a European village, but there are also television sets and washing machines, and big bottles of Slavic wine for anniversaries and such occasions as when their boys graduate from college.

Between them, the French natives and the Adriatic newcomers have achieved masterly techniques for tracking the schools of pale Gulf shrimp and for working over the oyster bottoms, where Mississippi and other coastal waters combine with the salty Gulf to provide ideal conditions for the shelled delicacies. Labors are long and not easy, but if all things work together, the reward may be good.

The Biloxi fleet—nearly one thousand trawlers—can be a stirring sight, as it plows through the glistening waters. On shore stand canneries, freezing plants and other processing factories, where ten thousand people make a living in one phase or another of the industry. Over all this, trouble has broken in the past, with workers

Gingerbread
"lighthouse"
among the trees

The tree-house
design for living
among the branches

and management firing furious charges and also an occasional hammer or other implement. For the present, peace has settled over the bay.

Biloxi seldom forgets that its base is a fishy one. Whenever the boats chug in, day or night, canneries let out a series of shattering blasts. When I first heard them, I thought it a signal of some disaster; new visitors have been known to run out in pajamas. Next to the fish, these guests have Biloxi's major attention. They are arriving by the growing thousands, and the town labors to keep them occupied: hotel tournaments, trips to the islands, fishing parties, Mardi Gras and, above all for some, Biloxi yacht racing that has won fame in other places, with the September Lipton Cup series, an annual midsummer regatta and other competition over a highly regarded yacht course.

In recent years the town has acquired a third major industry— the military. Here the Keesler Air Force Base operates at full tilt with some eighteen thousand men, most of them in training for various phases of electronics, including radar and radio. At the moment new millions are to be spent for work relating to the handling and tracking of missiles and anti-missiles.

Many of the boys tear off for New Orleans at the first chance; others, happily for Biloxi, stay and eat, drink, buy and indulge in other off-the-base activities. Frictions arise out of the presence of shifting masses of Air Force people, taking over space in the city limits, but any suggestion that the town lose Keesler brings a groan. As for the Air Force men, one shrugged as he enjoyed fried shrimp and Scotch on the rocks with a date from Ocean Springs.

"It could be a lot worse. Suppose this was Dry Creek in my home state?"

Along much of the Gulf, old paths twist among overhanging trees, with irregular narrow streets in a southern European pattern. . . . All such scenes are absent in Biloxi's great rival, Gulfport, a brisk "American town," unlike the more leisured ones about it. At the start of the twentieth century Gulfport had hardly been born; it came out of planned parenthood between Southern lumber and Northern money.

For years long-leaf pine grew thickly over southern Mississippi, but the land lacked roads or other outlets. In the late 1880s a band of Southerners headed by Judge William H. Hardy started a rail line through the area, only to see the venture collapse. Then Captain Joseph T. Jones of New York revived it as a warmly personal project;

he put up his own office building, hotel and bank, and he built a pier into the Gulf for ships to meet his railroad.

Gulfport burst into being with a flourish. Streets were straight, wide, long; the town had no Creole cottages, no houses on stilts along the water. The place looked like what it was, an engineer's project moved from blueprint to the sandy soil. Sawmills sprang up along the railroad; a lumber rush was on, and in one year the town sent out more yellow pine than any other port on earth. Then came trouble, when a storm knocked down about a quarter of all the Mississippi timber and the town's economy trembled; gradually, too, the piny woods were overcut, and Gulfport had to discover other means of support or die.

It found them, drawing cotton warehouses, compresses, factories, improving its superior ship channel, extending its pier. Today Gulfport is the area's ever-expanding business center; but meanwhile its trees have grown, its vines and flowers thickened, and "the coast" has crept about it.

Closer to Alabama lies Pascagoula, in part a drowsing old settlement, in another part one of the coast's most roaring shipyards—and also center of an ancient phenomenon and a legend. The Duchess de Chaumont, of Louis XIV's court, received the original land, and in 1718 its first fort was built: a small, simple structure of moss, mortar and crushed shells. After many vicissitudes, it remains with ancient walls, a foot and a half thick, and roof held up by heavy hand-hewn timbers.

For generations Pascagoula has been a fishing center, a shipping and shipbuilding town. Natives wryly admit that it won quiet fame during Prohibition for producing "the best damn rum-running boats in the world," which no government agent could catch—until the government also turned to Pascagoula. The town achieved new fortune when the Ingalls corporation arrived in 1930, eventually becoming the biggest shipbuilding organization in the Deep South and Mississippi's largest industry. This group produced the world's first all-welded seagoing vessels, and is now going ahead with nuclear-powered Navy submarines.

Pascagoula also has a "Singing River." Centuries ago the pioneers heard a mystic humming which began deep in the water. "You stand there," a native says, "and lil by lil it come to you, like a thousing voices whisperin' under they breats. It's best jus' aroun' dark and in summer, and it get' louder till it beats in your ears and seems like

Egret at ease: the sign means what it says

Philosophy near
Pass Christian:
the contemplative
Brahman bull

And always, waiting,
lurking, or merely resting . . .

it's right under you." Many have guessed at the explanation: a trick of underwater currents, marsh gas, movement of sand.

Old Pascagoulans tell a simple tale. A young chieftain of the kindly Pascagoula tribe fell in love with a girl of the Biloxi, who thought themselves a sort of master race among the Indians. The girl escaped to the Pascagoulas, who fought a battle with the enemy and lost. Faced with harsh defeat, the whole tribe, with the young lovers before them, went to the river. Hands interlocked, they walked forward, singing until they were gone; and their voices can still be heard. . . .

It is a coast of many other stories, many other sights.

At Long Beach a tall oak bears a high white platform with stairs leading from below—"Friendship Oak," under which the poet Vachel Lindsay held classes at Gulf Park College. At Pass Christian stands the "Dixie White House," a plantation style of building where Woodrow Wilson visited in 1913. Biloxi has a famous lighthouse which had two attendants, mother and daughter, for sixty-two years. When Lincoln died, a sorrowing admirer painted it black in mourning.

Nearby is the "Ring of the Oak." The legend says that an Indian girl fell in love with the son of an enemy tribe. (This apparently was a popular habit on the coast.) Her father, still another chief of the Biloxi, shook his head; she would never marry him until a ring grew in that tree over there. A few hours later a hurricane twisted about the oak, and in the morning the father discovered a clear ring, still to be seen. . . .

For many, however, the place which brings the greatest curiosity is Beauvoir, near Biloxi, where Jefferson Davis spent the last dozen years of his life. A proud, tight-tempered man, his nerves often strained, and one convinced always of the correctness of his own views, Davis had passed harsh years as President of the Confederacy. He had watched every hope fail; he had known the taste of gall. For a time after capture, he had been shackled in a Union cell.

Then Jefferson Davis had come to a high and beautiful house, provided by the kindness of a woman who admired him. He made a small payment on Beauvoir, and eventually she left it to him. The one-time President had land but little money; friends deceived him gently and made advances from his "earnings." With his wife, Varina, he walked about the gardens at Beauvoir, stared at the Gulf, and remembered, and with her help he wrote his *Rise and Fall of the Southern Confederacy.*

He must have suffered hours of unspoken bitterness, this unbend-

Beauvoir: last home of the Confederacy's President

Shadowed interior at Beauvoir: the daughter
could not marry her Northern lover

ing old man in dark coat and Panama hat. When his story appeared it was legalistic, lacking the warmth and humanity which another might have given it. And yet he spoke eloquent and moving words a year before he died, when he addressed young men along the Coast:

> The past is dead, let it bury its dead, its hopes, its aspirations . . . Let me beseech you to lay aside all rancor, all bitter, sectional feeling and take your places in the ranks of those who will bring about a consummation devoutly to be wished for—a reunited country.

Jefferson Davis left Beauvoir soon afterward, to die in the home of Judge C. E. Fenner in New Orleans. One daughter, Margaret, married a man from Colorado and went to live there. Another, the poised and handsome Winnie, had a less happy life. Before her father's death a New Yorker proposed to her. As has often been said, Winnie loved him, yet, since he was of that other region, she could not marry him. After her father's death he proposed a second time and, according to the story told here, she accepted him. But her Southern friends protested so strongly that she ended the engagement and died soon afterward.

On my last trip to Beauvoir I stopped for an hour in the room that is a sad little shrine to Winnie Davis, with the jewels and robe she wore as Queen of Comus during the New Orleans Mardi Gras. A little after that she was gone. Beauvoir became a home for Confederate veterans and their wives; some of the men married Northern girls after the war. Now they have all gone, too, and Beauvoir is a memorial. Like so many others who visit here, I reflected for a time about Jefferson Davis and his daughter, who gave up the man she loved. . . .

Creole city from the river edge, with steamer *President* at the dock

New Orleans, Where It's Different

viii

"IN LOUISIANA," a man will say ironically or in simple statement, "it's never the same as in other places. And in New Orleans—well, it's even less so."

On the Gulf Coast and in New Orleans the background, the people are different in a dozen ways. Much of the reason for that difference is the Mississippi, which makes Lower Louisiana a peculiar battleground of soil and water, between the Gulf and the river. Here is the land's farthest extension out of the central coast, an oddly shaped series of projections which have puzzled many men.

As the Mississippi curves downward to the Gulf, century after century, it deposits half-liquid earth in a lengthening advance into the blue water. At the same time, in a way that few understand fully, the river's soil presses upon the area about it, like a giant hand, shifting the balance of the region. Meanwhile the Mississippi changes;

over the centuries it has taken several courses through Louisiana, moving east and west about an expanse of several hundred miles, creating several great deltas. Thus a war of the elements goes on, in a wide field of conflict.

Louisiana's coastline, fantastically tattered and indented, is fifteen hundred miles long; only Florida's and California's are longer. On the Gulf edge the salt water beats steadily in against the land. At few points on the shores below New Orleans is there a dependably dry place for a sizeable settlement. A series of outposts, often changing with the years . . . those are all. The salt marshes reach far inland, as flatlands of eternal green, cut by twisting rivulets, inlets, bayous that extend like spider webs, and lagoons in which the bowl of the sky is endlessly reflected. To the Gulf side stretch barrier beaches of fine white sand and occasional high shell ridges on which rise groves of oaks to which Louisianians give the name of *chênières*. *Grand Chênière, Chênière au Tigre* . . . On them and other scattered spots French America holds sway.

This is a region where accented English may be the only English; where men use the mother tongue which their *mères* and *pères* and *grandpères* taught them. It is a place, too, where the volatile temperament rules, where a fury may break in a moment, then go just as quickly. Physically it may be primitive: a tiny hut or a cluster of huts at the edge of a shining lake, and nothing more. But it can be a scene of serene contentment, of a quiet, unquestioning happiness. Whatever *le Bon Dieu* will give . . . that will be enough.

Gradually, as the marshes continue inland, they grow a bit higher, the water becomes brackish and eventually fresh. In time there are swamps, their liquids stained with the seepings of the earth. These are brooding areas, their silence broken only by the whirring of bird wings, the plop of an occasional furred animal, the trickle and splash of a current.

The Gulf land of Louisiana is a part of America in the remaking, moving irregularly from earth to liquid or something that has a little of each element. At one point mats of water hyacinths spread over shallow ponds; dead vegetation will sink, thickening the water while other growths climb upon the pads above. From upward and downward the amount of liquid is lessened, and then there is land or a reasonable resemblance to it.

Yet meanwhile pressure from the alluvial Mississippi soil may make the area begin to drop. The winds and Gulf waters are also at work; in a bad hurricane both may rip and tear, pull away what took years to build. Here and there, as in Plaquemine and St. Bernard parishes below New Orleans, grounds that once supported stalks of sugar cane are now under water. A small cemetery that stood near the end of an island above the Gulf has been lost in the water, only the tip of a tombstone forlornly showing over the waves.

"But me, I don' care so much," a light-hearted housewife shrugs. "Down by *ma cousine's* house, they say the lan' grow two hundred yard in they' mem'ry. They raisin' pig' where they once hunt' crab'. So what?" Meanwhile the people of this Lower Louisiana live in a teeming fertility of vines that grow too thickly, of palmettoes and willows and creepers that seem almost to devour their terrain. About them the air, land and waters are thick with animal and insect life, swarming, insistent; and here is one of the New World's heaviest areas of birds, living in government refuges, stopping for the winter or for short rests, before their plunging flights across the Gulf to the south.

The capital of this broad region is New Orleans, though not many of its people realize its full ties to the deep water. The Creole town lies one hundred twenty or so miles away, along the winding Mississippi, and many Orleanians have never beheld the Gulf. Yet if it were not for the spot's comparative closeness to the blue waves, the city would not be there at all.

The early Spaniards stared at the Louisiana shores but did not stay. The eighteenth century had almost dawned, when Iberville and Bienville beheld the strange barriers of broken trees and other deposits about the Mississippi's mouth and made France's original settlements on the coast to the east. Going up the river, they came upon a stretch of land in a semicircular turn of the stream, and here they established their *Nouvelle Orléans*. It gained slowly because of dissensions, storms and floods; that it survived at all was a miracle. The town had a Gallic existence on several levels: a high life for its bewigged masters, with wines and furniture imported from Paris, and a more casual, often rowdy style among their subjects.

Outside New Orleans the Louisianians took occasional places along the lower river, along the sandy shores and at the precarious entryways from the Gulf, with their sand bars to trap the unwary pilot. At this point of meeting between the river and the salt waters the colonists had a navigation problem that never ceased to plague them. Then, in the 1760s, Spain took Louisiana and the high-tempered Orleanians rebelled. "They were the first American colonials to rise up against their masters," the New Orleanian tells you, and

One part land, two parts water: the Mississippi winds to the Gulf

Two parts land, one part water: New Orleans in the river's bend

indeed they were. But the revolution was brief and effectively crushed by the new dons.

The town saw successive upheavals and suffered the scars of repeated fires that wiped out most of its houses. These conflagrations had a marked result. The New Orleans that sprang up again had not a French style but a Spanish one: fanlight windows, stuccoed walls, interior courts or patios, ironwork grilles and balconies. And among the people a distinctive type evolved—the Creoles, descendants of the French and Spanish. (In New Orleans the term does not mean Negro.) Although they had something of the eye and air of languorous Spain, the Creoles stayed French in their hearts; while they accepted Madrid, they never forgot Paris.

Under Spain Louisiana took another new population which would transform the Gulf edges, the marshes and *prairie tremblante,* the the quaking prairie beyond New Orleans. From Nova Scotia arrived thousands of the Acadians, those victims of international hatreds, and they went to the unfilled rural sections. They gave their names and fixed their characters on the bayou edges. Good, hard-working people, they lacked the sophistication of the Orleanians, but they dominated much of the area. The city Creole, the country Cajun . . . they became the two sides of the Louisiana coin. Each, one directly, the other indirectly, helped fix the special tone of the laughter-loving capital.

Gradually, no matter what the Spanish rulers thought, a new pressure increased upon New Orleans: that of the thousands of Americans, who faced it from Kentucky and Tennessee and other territories above the Gulf. With their new freedom from England, they were spreading themselves in a leaping movement across the South. They had furs, grain and other produce, and a determination to send them to the sea. For that purpose there was one major outlet—New Orleans—and the "Kaintocks," as the Creoles called them, were of a mind to use it.

The Spaniards had scant sympathy with queer ideas such as free trade and access to the sea. They put up obstacles, made confiscations, and yet they could not halt the tide. American produce reached the Gulf and soon the Americans followed it. When Napoleon took Louisiana from the weakening Spanish and sold it to the Americans, he was, in a sense, merely anticipating history; almost certainly the Anglo-Saxons would have engulfed the area after a time. In any case the purchase was the world's biggest real estate deal, involving land for half a dozen empires at less than a nickel an acre.

As much as any single event, it assured America's unbroken progress as a continental power.

Did the Orleanians greet democracy with a cheer? Instead, most of them groaned or lifted noses at the barbarian newcomers; to them the United States meant brawling, unshaven flatboatmen, celebrating the end of their long ride down the river by belching insults at the townfolk. At the same time many Americans felt dismay: All that land, so much bigger than the original nation, and those peculiar Louisiana people, with their foreign manners and who knew what in their French minds!

Legal affairs had to be conducted in two and three languages. Who, monsieur, understood this funny American tongue? Agents in the Gulf fringes blinked at the nationalities they encountered: Spanish, Italians, Germans, Acadians, Swiss, Middle Europeans, a few Orientals, in a gumbo that thickened wherever they turned. And in New Orleans two cities developed, the Creole one below the dividing line of Canal Street, the American area above it. The first was the closely built locality of stucco-fronted, iron-balconied houses on narrow Royal, Bourbon and other squares, flush with the sidewalk or *banquette,* behind which residents lived with their back to the world. The American section was the more open one of separated houses with gardens and lawns; here were another people, leading other lives. French *grandmères* shrugged when asked if they had ever gone above Canal. Why should they? *This* was New Orleans!

Only a decade later events in and about the Louisiana Gulf startled the nation. Privateering and piracy had long been part of the way of life on the coast from Florida to Texas; nowhere did they flare up in so bizarre a fashion as in the marshes beyond New Orleans, about Barataria and Grand Isle.

Throughout the French and Spanish days, smugglers and corsairs had operated with occasional interruptions. The locale, cut by so many openings, was one in which a man could lose himself in a minute or two and hide for years. When the United States outlawed importation of slaves, while permitting bondage to continue, a rich incentive was provided for expanded illegalities. Thousands of dark men and women were brought in, and in New Orleans a number of bankers, lawyers and merchants served as more or less respectable "front men" for shady individuals at the Gulf shores.

Of these mixed crews of mixed men, Jean and Pierre Lafitte were the most flamboyant. They carried on a highly organized business in and around the Barataria section below New Orleans, using one or two Gulf islands as headquarters. In time the Lafittes' operations became bolder than ever and the American Government was moving in on them when, late in 1814, the British fleet approached Louisiana. Into New Orleans came the unprepossessing Andrew Jackson, a man regarded without enthusiasm by the Louisianians who met him. Could this lank *Américain* be a real soldier? The American frontier fighters, arriving day by day, shook their heads. How could they win under these conditions?

Out in the Gulf the powerful British force sent a messenger with a proposition to Jean Lafitte. If he helped them he would be protected and made a Captain in England's service. The pirate considered; he had mixed motives for any choice he might make. Nevertheless he turned to the American side. And all at once New Orleans rallied behind Jackson, in a soaring wave of emotion against the invaders.

Scoring a surprise, the English made a quick advance through the bayous—and one of the miracles of Gulf history happened. Unused to the swampy terrain, the redcoats blundered forward to be picked off by riflemen, blasted to the earth by Jackson's big guns, demoralized by the strangeness of their situation. On the green fields of Chalmette, below New Orleans, Europe's most superb military forces fell before the amateurs of the American South. The city had been saved; pirates became respectable for a time and the conquering hero of Chalmette, like other soldiers before and after him, eventually went to the White House.

But for years afterward operations by shady individuals continued along the islands of the Gulf, and meanwhile in New Orleans the Creoles and Americans still competed for trade and ascendency. Gradually the energetic new arrivals were to win, yet the town still did not lose its spice. Strangers gaped at a gaudy show on the levee: steamboats that swung up and down the river; plump country planters, levee-edge dealers in suspect undertakings; lines of slaves among the cotton bales and molasses barrels, and the often-whispered-about quadroons and octoroons, those seductive women who formed a special class, with white men as their "protectors" in little houses at the city's borders.

It was America's least American outpost. Duels over fancied insults, fights among the hard-bitten river-front boatmen, carousings that shocked visitors from New England . . . Some called it a worldly hell, and certain critics appear to have confused the town with Dante's Inferno. It was probably not so wicked as they portrayed it, but it was never Binghamton or Hartford. "Everybody" came here: Adelina Patti for her sensational first American appearance; Mark Twain and Thackeray; Abraham Lincoln and the awkward genius, Stonewall Jackson; Lafayette and Lola Montez.

Upon the town there tumbled a wealth such as it had never imagined: staples from the advancing plantations, produce of the West, imports from Europe. Thomas Jefferson had predicted: "The position of New Orleans certainly destines it to be the greatest city the world has ever known." For a time it appeared that the Creole-American town would go beyond New York. Then, slowly, a slight comparative decline. It was not simply "the war," which Orleanians, like other Southerners, blame for too many things. It was, instead, a combination of several factors.

As early as the 1830s New York, Pennsylvania and Maryland were cutting canals to divert Western goods. Ominously railroads began to change the old pattern of north-south water traffic. New Orleans heeded only a little, for it was concentrating happily on the ever-higher totals of cotton, as the Cotton Capital of Dixie. In 1861, Louisiana seceded; from the Gulf, a year later, there moved a new enemy, and this time there was no Andrew Jackson to defend the city.

Heading the Union fleet was Farragut, who had spent years as a boy in New Orleans. Sixty miles below the city were the powerful Forts Jackson and St. Philip, one on each bank, and many considered them impregnable. The first stood pentagon-shaped, surrounded by a moat, with two brick faces to the Mississippi. Fort St. Philip, dating back to the Spanish days, was a quadrangle, heavily armed. From river bank to river bank there stretched a barrier of logs and old schooners, chained together. Approaching from the Gulf, Farragut's forces had fifty vessels, including mortar schooners capable of deadly fire. Behind the forts the Confederates had their smaller fleet in reserve. After anchoring at Ship Island, the Union ships rolled up to the river mouth, and the first one or two promptly stuck in the mud. For weeks the commander ordered further soundings and then, following a minutely prearranged plan, pressed up the Mississippi. In this area of flat wetlands, bronzed trappers and fishermen blinked at the naval monsters; at the forts children ran forward to watch, and one girl died in the crossfire. Stripping down his vessels, the Union commander went through six days of continuous bombardment of the forts, firing six thousand shells. The Confederates blasted back and still held on.

In the stalemate Farragut shifted tactics. During the night the Unionists slipped up to the river barrier and broke a gap. Then just before 2 A.M. the Federal force steamed through the opening and a raging battle broke; ship fired on ship and sometimes it was hard to tell friend from enemy. Farragut's flagship caught fire, and he cried out in anguish. Was everything over?

All at once the way lay open, and the Federals pressed triumphantly on, past fortifications at Chalmette, those fields at which Jackson had won in 1815. New Orleans was helpless, and the Confederacy would be cut in two. Behind Farragut rode another Unionist whom New Orleans was to hate more than any man at any time: Ben Butler. Ironically Butler's father had served under Jackson in saving New Orleans on that earlier occasion.

In the years after the war the city's docks lay idle and cotton arrived in meager lots. Equally grim became the situation at the river mouths, where the Mississippi silted up; as ships grew increasingly larger, they had ever more trouble in getting from the Gulf. Unless something were done there, New Orleans might be doomed. The answer was a vital effort: building mighty jetties of rock and concrete along South Pass, in order to force the river to scour out a deepened channel into the water. The scheme worked; this revolution at the Gulf made it possible for the city to come back. Slowly the tough old town revived; triumphantly it achieved a new front rank.

Today an ever-thickening line of shipping moves in and out of the Gulf from New Orleans, carrying more goods to and from more places than ever before. Again it is the country's second port in dollar value of foreign trade and the prime gateway between the resurging Mississippi valley and the world. Her port facilities, remade from end to end, cover twelve miles of richly efficient deepwater terminals and operational points, and work has begun on a new channel giving direct, shortened access to the Gulf.

One by one the town has beaten the problems that dogged its history: the threat of tropical disease, of flood, of ingrowing lethargy. And yet at the same time New Orleans is largely *sui generis,* a living place in its own particular image.

Born in 1910, I grew up in a Creole city that lost but slowly some of its relics of a highly colored past. Great side-yard cisterns still caught rainwater; deep, sometimes noisome, gutters lined the *banquette* edges. Along many streets I stumbled over cobblestones and flagstones, and like others I looked in wonder at graying Greek Revival houses in areas that were becoming new commercial blocks above Canal Street. In my early years all beds—from old four-posters with the stamp of Seignouret, Mallard or other masters, down to mere cots—needed mosquito bars. Anyone who did not have such netting about him rose with bloated face following a night of restless pain. And after practically any heavy or medium rain Negro boys made small fortunes by holding wooden boxes, so that people could cross the overflowed ditches.

An early burning memory is of the September hurricane of 1915. In less than one day 8.36 inches of water covered the town. (In two weeks New Orleans received nearly 23 inches.) Just before the height of the howling winds, we left our house for the refuge of a sturdy neighborhood market. My mother's main concern appeared to be that our piano would float away. It did not, nor did the house.

Although my family is Scots-Irish, it did not strike me as unusual that half the people around us spoke with a French accent, and that in some houses I visited the older members knew no English. Trips to the French Quarter with my elders were events: the odd houses, crowded tightly together, dark little antique shops with cameo rings and family pictures, clothes that hung between balconies of once elegant residences, now rooming houses below Jackson Square; the dinginess of the great old Ursuline Convent, the sadly worn look of the tall red-brick Pontalba Apartments.

Here and there the Quarter had a Latin air, with old men dozing in the sun and barefoot children at play in the courtyards under the flapping laundry. Years later I recognized much the same scene when I first saw Naples. For the French section had become to a degree Italian. Thousands had arrived from southern Italy to fill the waterfront, the schools and churches, and I knew dozens of Palermos and Salvaggios.

Other friends had names like D'Abadie and Livaudais, among them a pair of maiden ladies who wore crinkly black blouses and plain black skirts and talked of the upriver plantation that the family had given up. With several such neighbors I went to the French Opera, once so glittering, now come on dusty times. To a seven- or eight-year-old, however, there was a glory about the cavernous structure with the dark hangings, the vast stage and the almost equally vast sopranos. Sometimes I slept after trying vainly to follow the inexplicable behavior with swords and stake-burnings. Yet I was still taken by the wonder of the scene, the lines of carriages, the yells of French and Italian devotees over a high C.

On the way we passed elderly Negro women in crisp gingham, carrying baskets from which they sold *"Plarines, plarines!"* These were pralines, those remarkable mixtures of brown sugar, pecans and French skill. I have never had one without asking for a second; or two, without inquiring for a third. With or without a praline, I walked quickly by the old "Haunted House" where people said Madame Lalaurie had tortured her slaves, and we continued on our way to the long open French Market with its heavy Spanish pillars and stretches of fruit, fish and meat—sometimes succulent, sometimes altogether too fishy or otherwise aromatic.

We children did not feel alarm, but only curiosity when we passed the enormous, decaying hulk of the St. Louis Hotel, with its copper dome and the spot, somewhere dimly inside, where "the slaves had been sold." Later I recalled a trip to the gleaming Sazerac bar, where artists of the mixing process prepared transcendant combinations of Bourbon, bitters and absinthe (a soupçon at the end), and to another place where patrons stood at an astonishingly long bar to sip Ramos gin fizzes—deceptive unions of cream, gin, egg white and other items. As a juvenile, I had to stand at or near the door; simply to be there was a glorious thing.

The docks and wharves were wonder spots of another kind, with a ripe redolence of coffee and bananas, of rope and muddy water. Today, whenever I walk in that vicinity, a breeze from the riverfront brings it all back. Vivid in other fashions were the two days that are combined, not illogically, in my mind: Mardi Gras and All Saint's.

Being Catholic, the Kanes took over much of the Creole absorption in the day of the dead. With French neighbors we visited the cemetery in advance, made certain that the graves or tombs were cleared of weeds, whitewashed or generally spruced up. On the holiday itself, a universal one here, we went in a family body to "pay our respects," also to observe who else had appeared and who had not; who had returned or not returned from the country for the occasion. It was a big, friendly affair, and not a greatly sorrowful one. On the way the children always got licorice sticks or chunks of striped peppermint. It was good to be in New Orleans.

And Mardi Gras! No child unfortunate enough to be brought up in another city could realize the steadily mounting tension as Carnival week approached; the first night parades, the hour or so of waiting for the shimmering floats behind the mules; the red-and-yellow illumination of the flambeaux, the joyful catching of trinkets tossed out by the masked figures to the cries of "Throw me something, Mister. Throw me something . . ."

Nightly there was the glory of the parades until the great day itself, when children woke first to call to the rest of the family and go forth as early as possible as Satans or junior lion-tamers. Mardi Gras was a marathon that left most of us dragging our feet or dozing in a chair, but while it was on it seemed a magnificent progression: day parades, the strutting Jefferson Buzzards in blackface, bands of shouting, jigging youths and maskers in twos and threes and twelves. Long before dark and the final shining parade, the young were ready for bed. For a long time the family made my face flush by recalling the way I cried, "Throw me something," then fell asleep just as the whistle came through the air.

In time there would be Carnival balls, a season which now begins around Christmas and goes on for many weeks, growing bigger with the years. New Orleans has changed, but Mardi Gras has never palled. . . . Through everything I never lost the conviction that this was a special place in the world. Meanwhile, without realizing it at the time, I watched New Orleans throw off one after another of its handicaps.

In one year before the Confederate War, yellow fever had taken ten thousand lives, a major portion of the population; now its threat has vanished. The harsh drainage problem ended, when the city installed one of the world's greatest system of pumps. To wipe out the danger of bubonic plague from rats brought by ships, New Orleans had an unprecedented hunt for rodents, with block-by-block inspections and rat-proofing of thousands of floors. And the Bonnet Carre spillway above the city holds a massive plug that may be pulled to drain off flood waters in years to come.

Today New Orleans persists as a place not yet planed down to the level of most other American cities—one in which the past walks at your elbow: a town of streets below Esplanade Avenue that open unexpectedly with a small house like a French provincial residence; of former servant quarters, softly repainted, half hidden behind lines of banana plants and glimpsed through an opening in a green gate; of institutions such as the unchanging oyster bars at which well-chilled oysters on the half shell have been handed forth for generations.

Whenever I have been away for some time I will head toward such an oyster place for a dozen or so of these inducements to well-being. Then a walk down Royal Street to glance into a private patio or two in which the tall trees provide a shaded, greenish light; a stop at an old-style Quarter bookshop like Harmanson's or the Plantation, and a large cup of *café au lait* at the French Market. Within sight of Jackson Square the roofs of the Cabildo and Presbytere rise in their unchanging outlines against the clouds.

Quarter figures go by: a thoughtful monsignor, a collector of duelling pistols, a recent Carnival queen who works nearby, a writer of twenty-two unpublished novels; a police official recently indicted by the grand jury; a gentle Negro nun; a Bourbon Street stripper, who may be the one named Redi Flame, or another whose act had

A good time was had by all thousands of them

her bathe five times nightly in "wine," who then announced she was "the cleanest girl in town."

Or it may be the girl with a duck, unleashed, waddling behind her. Or a gleaming bartender who can recite the name of every vice-president. Or, until very recently, the restaurant owner who liked diamonds and wore them practically everywhere—from the frames of his eyeglasses to his tooth fillings, cuff links, shirt buttons, tie pins, belt and a well-studded zipper, its catch in the shape of a V for Victory.

"Ah, *comment ça va?*" someone will call. "Where *you* been while we working people work?"

Then I know I am home.

Mardi Gras: float bearing Rex, Joseph M. Jones,
hails Queen Ainslie Dinwiddie
ALLEN JOHNSON

Steamboat come to land: gingerbread house
in New Orleans-Arabi area

Old survivor: Magnolia plantation on the lower west bank

Movement on the bayou: Intracoastal canal to Texas

Movement on the Mississippi: upriver to St. Louis

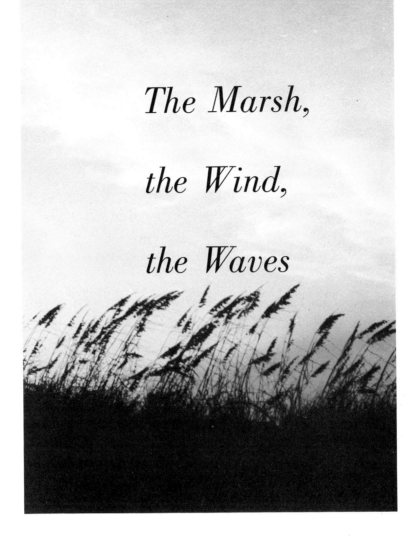

The Marsh,

the Wind,

the Waves

ix

TO the south and west of New Orleans stretch the lands of the other Louisianians whose ways are directly shaped by the Gulf. Some live on bits and ridges of land that extend like threads from the city; until recently others could be reached only by water, and a number are still isolated in the same fashion. At varying distances above the deep water a series of towns and cities advances across Lower Louisiana to the Texas border.

Even more than New Orleans itself, this region is French America. In most cases the coloration is brunette, the accent as piquant as the flavoring of the food, and the rule of life a calm resignation to whatever the day or night will bring.

"*Eh, bien.* It do you no good to fret. What gon' happen, gon' happen, now ain' it?"

To stay for a time in any of these places, especially the smaller ones, is to absorb their philosophy. In the words of one of my city friends, "You learn to shrug or you break into pieces." Few south Louisianians that I have met are inclined to break into pieces. Yet they can also be mercurial, their moods changing in a moment, and stubborn.

Often they laugh at newcomers who proceed to advise them about methods of roadbuilding in their area, or about fishing or the weather.

"Don' tell me," they may say with a grimace. "*Ma famille,* he been here since befo' your *Grandpère* born." Regarding the winds and the waves the natives are particularly adamant, and generally they are right in what they believe on these important subjects. But, as we shall see, not always right. . . .

The names echo the nature of the people. Directly down the Mississippi are Happy Jack, Venice, The Jump; to the west, Breaux Bridge, Labadieville, Paincourtville.

"We pick they name' as the spirit move us," a stout older citizen made it clear. As often as not, there is Gallic humor or shrewd observation in the selection of a title, which alters with the time and the people.

Changes are developing swiftly throughout this land. Into even the meager villages, television and deep-freezes penetrate, often taking their places beneath calendar likenesses of the Blessed Virgin. Certain teen-agers take on the mannerisms of the Presleys and the Sal Mineos, yet with a Cajun accent and touch. But for scattered thousands, young and aged, the old ways persist.

Annually they go out, one foggy morning after another, to set their lines over the spongy green wastes in which they labor to trap furred animals that give them part of their living. Despite ups and downs in muskrat catching, Louisiana continues a fur empire of the New World. Daily men and boys will follow the lines, rising before dawn and working through the day, poling their way in pirogues through watery passages, sinking to their knees or lower in the tricky terrain.

There will be time for coffee or a thick stew in a tar-paper hut at the edge of a marsh. But they will try to lose not more than a few minutes here, a few there. They are struggling against a deadline. "An' if this be a good year, the nex' may be bad-bad," in the words of an ancient near Thibodaux. In these areas near the Gulf nobody rests; the women and the girls use their skills for hours, early and late, over the skins on the drying racks. When I joined one family, a short time ago, I lasted four days, then went home to recover.

In spring the same family may hunt crabs with "trot lines" and baited nets marked by wooden floaters in the shallow water. Once more the men move from spot to spot, lifting nets, emptying them, dropping them back. Into the hampers fall the lively, dark-backed, light-clawed catch that require a certain adroitness in handling. At this task, like any city man, I proved worse than useless to my Gulf-side friends. I got back with four swollen fingers and a throbbing back.

Again, the marsh man will hunt for the special crab, the soft shell for which the nearest dealer or restaurant will pay well. This one must be taken after he has outgrown his old outer cover and worked out of it, and before his frame has hardened again. It is even more taxing, back-bending labor, as I discovered when I tried to assist Cajun friends near the marsh. But anyone who has tasted the succulent result, a broiled "buster crab," will know how well the effort is worth it.

For still others there is the gathering of a crop planted and harvested much like the green things of the field—the oyster. An oyster-gathering "Tocko" or Yugoslavian near Ostrica in the Delta below New Orleans allowed me to go along, but only to watch.

"These thing' too valuable to let even a frien' fool aroun' wit'," he made clear.

The oyster needs a certain amount of fresh water, "an' no mo' at all"; a certain amount of salty flow, "an' no mo' at all." The oyster-man sows shells, uses long oyster tongs to take up some of them for inspection and moves them from one bed to the other, sampling, shifting, experimenting. They have a final destination, one of those ancient and honorable oyster bars of New Orleans or Morgan City, Lafayette or Houma.

Additional marsh men, like some we have met at Biloxi and elsewhere, follow a more distant, more elusive crop, the "big shrimp" in the Gulf. From Morgan City and other points along the Louisiana shore the shrimp boats ride out to hunt this jumbo type ("big like your hand, or bigger"), so that they may cover most of a plate.

There are other part-time occupations: the pulling of moss from the trees to be sold for stuffing of mattresses or furniture; the catching or wrestling (with bare hands) of alligators, when the elusive creatures can be tracked to their haunts; the operation of motor boats through areas in which they are the only vehicles to be seen for hours at a time. Here and there children go to school by water, and a trip to a moving picture house means a ride on the water. ("If you ain' got no boat, you jus' stay home, tha's all.")

To travel over this region is to see a Franco-Southern land, varying in a hundred ways from other parts of America. From New Orleans,

Bellechasse and its ancient bell: Judah Benjamin was the master

Contrast: Seven Oaks plantation house among the oil tanks

Bayou Des Allemands: tranquil water,
tranquil people, tranquil fishing

Bayou Des Allemands:
railroad station
on stilts

down the same east bank of the river, the road passes the old Creole plantation area and Andrew Jackson's fields of Chalmette, now partly occupied by Kaiser Aluminum. And there are striking brick ruins of Versailles, a once-famous estate offering one of the sights of the region, a majestic double line of oaks. Then, fifty miles below New Orleans, at Pointe a la Hache, the road ends, and below begins the marsh that borders the winding river to the Gulf.

On the west bank below New Orleans stands Bellechasse, the long-neglected columned house of Judah P. Benjamin, the high Confederate who escaped through Florida to England. Near Junior and Venice are stretches where lilies are grown as crops among orange groves. Then there are Buras, where French, Spaniards and Yugoslavians have lived side by side, and Boothville and The Jump, where the river once cut through the land.

Here the levees fall away, and the last points of settlement down the Mississippi must be reached by water at Pilottown, Burrwood and Port Eads. In a setting of nesting pelicans and slowly flying gulls the river goes out to sea, pouring its silty water into the universal blue waves. Before then the land has sunk lower, lower, to nothing at all; yet the river still maintains its identity far out in the waves, its pale brown current pressing forth, until at last it dissolves in a mixed area of flying fish and skimming birds.

West from New Orleans, over the Long Bridge, the highway leads through Paradis to Raceland and the warm Cajun waterway, Bayou Lafourche. To the south another road continues downward past fishing boats and oil fields to Chênière Caminada and Grand Isle, former pirate retreat, now a place of endless camps, endless visitors and an abandoned government fort in the distance.

Up at Raceland alternate routes go to Thibodaux and Houma, each a center of bayou netways and industries, then on to Morgan City and Berwick Bay, heart of many waters, including the powerful Atchafalaya River, which has threatened at times to divert the main flow of the Mississippi along this shorter route to the Gulf.

Through Morgan City the main road advances to ancient New Iberia, with its celebrated plantation house, Shadows on the Teche; St. Martinville, the "Petit Paris" of earlier days and a site connected with the story of Evangeline; Avery Island, with Jungle Gardens and Bird City, which did much to save the egrets for America, and capital of the tabasco pepper industry.

Here, also, are Abbeville, old French town and entry place to a wide marsh region; Lafayette, heart of the Cajun prairie land, where buggies are still a popular method of transportation; Crowley, the capital of rice, in a setting of glistening green fields, and Lake Charles, the bustling city of western Louisiana, where the French locale shades into Texas—a town of Acadian accents, a hint of the speech of the Lone Star state, and an occasional ten-gallon hat.

Only in recent years has southwestern Louisiana—this region of the Gulf and the earth that merges with it—been recognized as a treasure place, one of the wealthiest in America. Under and about the moist soil lie riches still incalculable in minerals and animal and sea life. Sulphur, chemicals, oils are pouring out in a steadily increasing flow; the play of oil has extended eastward from Texas, and the Gulf area of Louisiana is an industrial empire in sudden development, with derricks dotting the land and marsh and reaching into the waters off shore.

Sharing in that new surge is Cameron Parish (County), one of the biggest in Louisiana, along the Gulf below Lake Charles. Despite its size, it has only an estimated six thousand people in the marshes, islands and *chênières* near the shore line. Nearly half of them are in the freshly prosperous town of Cameron, a mile-long stretch of ground at a point close to where the Calcasieu River meets the Gulf.

Few Americans had heard of Cameron until the summer of 1957, when it became a name for horror around much of the world. Late August or September is the usual hurricane time along the Gulf. Toward the end of June there was only a slight concern when the New Orleans Weather Bureau carried warnings of "Audrey," a disturbance in the waters. Most of the original settlers of little Cameron, largely French, were contented on this day of June 26, and so were those at Grand Chênière, Creole and other nearby points. Until a few years earlier, Cameron could be reached only by a boat, which came three times a week from Lake Charles; now a road connected it with the rest of the state.

The winds grew stronger, swaying trees and rattling windows. The clouds darkened and Gulf waves slapped against the outer grasses. Newcomers, largely Texans and other Anglo-Saxons, were alarmed, and several hundred of them began to leave, along with some of the French. Most of the natives shrugged and later they recalled their words: "I've seen worse." "It won' be so bad." A few maintained that the Weather Bureau did not make the disturbance "sound bad enough, or we'd of go." Another day went by; offshore most of the oil company workers left their rigs and headed for land. The sky became blacker, the water more agitated; out in the Gulf a mighty column of wind whirled forward, churning the sea, sucking in wooden fragments and other debris as it went.

After midnight a number of Cameron men remained up, and fifty or so stood before the school building, when one of the "new people," a mechanic, rode by and cried to them. "Get in your cars— hang on the top if you don't have room. Get out of here!" Only five or so heeded, and went with him. Most people returned home, old and young, to be with their families. Although some slept, the rest stayed awake, talking uneasily, reassuring one another that things would not turn out badly.

But the marsh waters were rising as they had never done before, an inch or two higher every few minutes. The Gulf, by which they had all lived, was moving in upon them. Galleries flooded, and currents seeped into kitchens and bedrooms.

Now and then a child cried out: "Mama, look the water."

Men and women argued what to do, and most climbed the stairs to upper floors or, if they did not have them, to the attic. Still the Gulf lifted steadily, steadily . . . One after another they realized that if worst came they would be caught in the attics "jus' like rats." Several pushed open vents to the roof; others, lacking such openings, told how they scurried down for axes and broke holes through which they shoved themselves and their families. As they stared down in the uncertain light, many felt fear at their throats. Already the whole town lay under water—four, five feet high and getting higher as they watched. In the courthouse people who could make their way there were clustered together; though it stood on the most elevated part of the settlement, even here the water eddied several feet above the floor.

Outside Cameron in his sturdily built new house the town's only doctor, young Cecil Clark, sat nervously with his wife, two daughters, a two-month-old baby and a housekeeper. Their two boys were visiting grandparents near Grand Chênière. He had had a broken night, delivering several children, and he was very tired. Now, two hours before dawn, a call came from Dr. Clark's small, twelve-bed hospital. He was needed there and he tried to drive in.

The doctor discovered the water was rising more swiftly than he had realized. Calling at a friend's house, he started again, the friend leading the way in his truck. The waves began to sweep them off the road; wading in waist-deep water, they returned to the friend's place.

Then, about dawn—twelve hours or so before the Weather Bureau had believed it would reach the area—"Audrey" struck.

Upon Cameron and other nearby points there roared a wind of 100 to 110 miles an hour that smashed and ripped, uprooted and tore at everything before it. At a hundred spots men and women of Cameron felt the shock. Practically every house caught the force of the howling elements. Small ones toppled over, throwing people into the water; others lost galleries, half the front, part or all of the roofs.

And with the wind, the tidal wave: a terrible, glistening green mountain of water that poured upon the cracked dwellings, keeling them over, sending them riding off, sinking, losing doors as they hit trees or rocked back and forth. In the wind or the water a huge oil barge was caught up like a paper boat, and two fifty-foot fishing vessels with them, and crashed upon the town, adding to the peril. Four fuel storage tanks were smashed, poles and powerlines knocked down.

Floors tilted as buildings lifted and fell crazily to the side. Screaming women fell into the water or rolled inside their houses, crying to their husbands, clawing for their children. The new house of Dr. Clark was heavily jarred. Already Mrs. Clark, like so many others, had gone to the roof, where she held her baby against her and the housekeeper clung to the two little girls. About them faint voices were calling through the rain and the slap of the water. Neither they nor any of the others could help; all were isolated, grasping whatever came to hand in the dim light.

Dr. Clark's house collapsed and the doctor's wife was swept away by the water—for twenty miles, she later discovered. Tossed by the cold waves, she held to her baby, until the child slid from her numb fingers. She screamed, looked around for the housekeeper and her two little girls. All of them were gone.

An engineer on a fishing boat waited in terror on the roof with his wife and three children. "Another house slammed into us. Ours fell apart and I grabbed on to the top and saw my wife do the same thing. She fell off, and my children did, too. I tried to get to them, and lost them."

Other men felt their houses disintegrate under them. "It fall jus' open, like the nail' was take' out." "Mine busted in two, like." They reached for their wives or mothers, and "watch' em' wash away, callin' to us." A few, clinging to doors or sections of walls, managed to pull two or three of their people to safety, only to have them slide off. "The win' took my boy. The las' I saw him he was with 'is arm aroun' a log and then it turned over and all there was, was the log."

Women, washed along on tables or parts of their galleries, stared as their babies dropped from the roof, moved a minute and sank under the surface. Girls in their teens managed to clasp the limbs of trees and draw a brother or sister up with them. From all sides they made out bobbing figures, heard screams close at hand. "But we couldn't do a thing. How could we?"

For those who survived, the terror had only begun. A woman floated for eight hours on a roof top. She, her husband and a nephew stayed there for a time, until the water washed them off once, then again. The first time the nephew, falling with her, caught her. "I was drowning with him, I think, till I saw him slip away. My husband grabbed me and got me back. We never saw my nephew again."

At the courthouse, as the winds abated, people came in, crying in despair, asking frantic questions. "What happen' to the Ledoux down the road?" "Anybody hear about my aunt and uncle?" Scores were bloodied; one boy had two broken legs, and a man was caught on barbed wire that ripped into his sides. He had been "hung up" until he managed to tear himself loose . . . Dr. Cecil Clark worked on and on in sockless shoes, wet trousers and dirty polo shirt, setting bones, painting wounds, giving shots and sedatives to the hysterical. By now he knew that his house was gone; now and then, when he had the time, he asked himself: Would any of his family be saved?

Dozens spoke to him. "Still ain' seen them, Doc." "No, none of 'em." He gave information, directed men around him, as "ham" radio operators sent out frantic messages. Some distance off six men had been tossed from a capsized oil rig and were clinging to life rafts, as they were to do for thirty-six hours. Relatives caught dazed women as they struggled in, and tried to restrain them when they made out mangled forms on stretchers.

Slowly the long hours passed and the sun came out. For miles about the area men and women were holding to trees, to bits of wood, or huddling on small strips of land about which the waters eddied. An eleven-year-old girl and a nine-year-old one, their seventy-seven-year-old grandmother and a middle-aged woman cousin hung upon a wall of their broken home, drifting about the marsh. There they remained for more than a day; the grandmother became very sick and fell from the raft several times, "but we always got her back."

As the sun brightened, the heat burned down on this party, as on many others, parching hands and faces. They could taste the brine and they yearned for water. "Then the raft fell apart and

Grandma went under." The girls pushed a big board to her, caught a smaller section of wood that floated by, "and all four of us held onto it with our bodies down in the water."

All about them they beheld a frightening sight. From everywhere snakes had appeared—deadly water moccasins among them. Approaching the rafts and fragments of wood, the snakes tried to slip upon them with the human victims. Desperate people beat off the reptiles with sticks, kicked at them, pushed them off. Great rats emerged from the marsh, emboldened or maddened, and some bit at the children.

On the earth ridges, colonies of animals clustered: rats, snakes, a few frightened dogs. As the waves came higher the animals formed a silent truce and huddled there, waiting. In most cases all were drowned; now and then, however, a dog managed to reach a family and whimpered for hours at their side.

A man who had lost three small children noticed that a fourth, who lived through the exposure, was "talking out of his head." A snake had struck at him, and the family could only watch helplessly. The boy died some hours later. "And now," said the father, "I got to go out and hunt for my babies' bodies."

Boats and trucks were leaving Lake Charles and other settlements. Helicopters swept over the area, and pilots stared in astonishment at the skeletons of the houses, at floating carcasses of animals—hundreds of cows washed to their death, and horses and dogs and people. So many, many people . . . Only slowly did the region realize the full extent of the tragedy. Men staggered in: A whole row gone up the road. The Bourgeois house, where there had been twenty—only the foundations.

Not for days would the total be known; it climbed to one hundred, 175, 250, to 500. Bodies were floating about singly, in twos and threes, corpses caught in the crotches of trees, or snagged by barbed wire. The drowned land gave up its dead by degrees; on the dry stretches, steaming in the sun, some still lay dying. Millions of mosquitoes winged about the more stagnant waters, and buzzards feasted as a sweet-sour stench rose over the desolation.

Roads had washed away in places; at others, stranded boats and litter held off traffic until bulldozers cleared the way. On patches of land men and women sat in silent despair, heads in hands. They had lost everything—houses, savings, families. At the courthouse and a few other gathering spots, someone went forward whenever a boat arrived. "You know where my Annette is? You see my two boys?"

In a canal a helicopter crew made out a clogged section, thick with bloated cows, and eight water-soaked human corpses among them. One rescuer saw the figure of a woman sitting at a window. Hurrying up, he found her there, caught against the sill; she, her husband and a baby had been drowned as they fought their way about.

Men talked in a dull monotone. "I'm looking for my sister and her chirren. Last time I saw them they was hanging onto a tree, with her holding her baby. He was ten months . . ." "I saved four people, but while I did it I lost my family. Yes, all of 'em." Near them lone dogs sat by broken rubble, all that was left of what had been their homes. A short distance off animals still swam feebly in the water, only their noses out of it; before long they would be dead.

Into Lake Charles went hundreds of the injured and homeless, to linger about a makeshift hospital in the McNeese State College gymnasium. In the hot, humid building, people wiped the perspiration from their faces and gazed dazedly about them. Children stood in rags, men in trousers that were all they had left. They told of a man who had come to Cameron to hunt his nieces, six and four. Stoically he looked down at a disfigured face.

"That's Glory Jean, I believe," and approached another form. "I think it's Dina. I'll get her brother, and he'll know."

A woman who had sat with arms folded for hours jumped when a five-year-old girl, muddied, bedraggled, arrived. "Baby, baby!" As she clutched the child she explained: "God be good to me. I give her up for dead." Another spoke: "Our place is jus' wiped out, but we got our family. And my lil boys, they been real good. Didn't cry once, even when we nearly drownded."

For some there was mixed word. Dr. Clark had lost his baby and both his little girls, but he learned that his wife had been located and soon she lay under treatment for shock and exposure. Yet others were silent, waiting alone for word of their families that never arrived. By this time new terrors had arisen: What food was left lay rotted, contaminated; water was risky and thousands were asking: "Can't I have jus' a swallow?" "These three girls ain't had water for a whole day, and look their dry lips."

Mass burials had to be made. Cranes lifted crude pine coffins into trenches, and priests said final words in the Acadian dialect. Above their muffled voices came cries: "Over a hun'red grave', jus' right here. Christ have mercy, Jesus have mercy . . ." Scores would never be identified. ("We'll never know just how many children this place has really lost.") For a time an ice house became the only possible storage place for other bodies that piled up, and then in the June heat these must also be disposed of. . . .

A few spoke glumly. "I won' go back there, never. Nothin' to go back to." Others groaned: "I will. Where else do I have to go?" After a time thousands returned to Cameron and started the slow, disheartening task of rebuilding from almost nothing. The Red Cross, of course, helped greatly, and so did many others. Some months later Dr. Clark was chosen by the American Medical Association as the country's outstanding family physician of the year. And as Christmas approached many Louisianians thought of the crippled locality. What kind of happy season would it be for Cameron?

Toys and gifts were collected throughout the state for a "flying sheriffs' posse," a venture labeled (cornily, alas) "Operation Toylift." On a day just before the holidays the distributors arrived. In the same courthouse that had witnessed so much misery, 850 boys and girls lined up to get apples and candy and dolls and trains.

Many of the young were orphans; others had lost most members of their families, but they seemed to laugh as easily, or almost as easily, as the children of other places. Families, many still living in tents, gathered for the occasion. Among them was a man, now boarding with friends, who had lost his wife, father and four young ones; this Christmas season he went to church for the first time since the disaster. And, it was said, people sang Christmas carols "who had not sung since June."

There were tears over many memories, but smiles had begun to return to Cameron. A few months later Cameron became the first American community to exceed its goal in the annual Red Cross drive. It said it wanted to "show its appreciation" for the nation's help.

Ready to make shrimp jambalaya
for the family supper

Like anybody else, nuns can enjoy a parade

Franklin, Louisiana:
Confederate soldier
stands over the
French country

Western Louisiana: We're getting toward Texas, podner

A boy and a bull calf: not hard if you
begin early with both

Near New Iberia: water-skiing along the banks of the Bayou Teche

Under the Texas coastal breeze, the cactus blooms

Gaudy,

but They

Got There

x

THE Texas Gulf Coast is the oldest Texas, the Texas that men of other countries first knew, and it is also the newest. Whatever may happen in the far-spread interior, it seems likely that the Gulf area will be increasingly *the* Texas of the twentieth century and also of the twenty-first.

The events that have occurred along this shore are largely the reason, or one of the main reasons, why New Yorkers, New Orleanians, Chicagoans, Memphians and the rest of the world talk about Big Texas, the Texas Approach, with anecdotes attached. From its first days the western Gulf provided a background for flamboyance, for characters with the will to do much as they liked.

Here the Gulf story comes full circle. For Texas provides a cast of big-talking, big-acting individuals who can match or overshadow Florida's lustiest. Did they make coastal Texas, or did it make them?

In any case, they have cast a gaudy reflection over their scene. Galveston, Corpus Christi, Houston . . . these older shore cities had origins that ranged from unprepossessing to raffish; they grew out of a frontier of mixed interests and confused loyalties.

There are, as Texans often note, a variety of Texases: the far desert stretches, the gaunt Panhandle, the central area, the Mexican borders and others. Between this warm, perspiring Gulf section, close to sea level, and the western lands of rocky and thorny shrub, and between the Gulf and most of the others, there exists a vast difference. In the main the Gulf Texan is not inclined to be taciturn; he is casual-tempered, talkative, fitted to his easier setting and easier climate.

In another way the area makes a circle, for, as in parts of Gulf Florida, this is a Latin-shadowed, Latin-brightened world. Soon after touching Florida, the early Spaniards continued along the coast to its lower western limits. In 1519 Pineda became the first of this procession of explorers, killers of Indians and hunters after gold. He drew the first known map of the Texas coast and halted for an exploration of the lushly tropical Lower Rio Grande. But it was at a point higher up the coast that other Spaniards soon made a dramatic landing near what would eventually be called Galveston Island.

Here a broken, parch-lipped party of Spaniards crept ashore in 1528—a fragment of the Narváez expedition, their crude ships wrecked along the shore. They quickly met a band of Karankawa Indians, tall nomads of the shore, who greased their faces and had a reputation for cannibalism. This time the Karankawas did not eat the Spaniards, but kept them prisoners. Not until seven years later did the white men slip away and drag themselves in a grim odyssey to the Gulf of California.

Understandably the party's leader, de Vaca, named the Galveston area "Malhado" (Misfortune). It won another title, after more than two centuries, when agents of Spain called it after Count Galvez, Viceroy of Mexico. More years went by, and it came to attention in the nineteenth century because of one of the most lurid episodes of coastal history. For decades it existed in a vacuum, claimed by both Spain and the United States. The uncertain situation provided an opening for shadowy border operators.

Mexico had broken out in revolt against Spain, and bands of adventurers came forward to act as privateers, or pirates, under Mexico's flag against the King's rich commerce. Word of the fine harbor at Galveston had spread among this gentry, and in 1816 Galveston became the sudden target of not one but three soldiers of varying fortune.

First came Louis Aury with a small fleet and plans to fortify the harbor. Aury had a checkered career. He was a hard-working would-be corsair, ready to do anything, cut any throat necessary to get what he wished. Sadly misfortune dogged him; he would always be a second-rate villain. He was joined by Francisco Mina, a sincere Spaniard interested in Mexico's freedom. They made an odd pair, he and Aury, but they held together as they started by water down the coast for a movement against the Spaniards. A quarrel broke out, Mina went on to die before a firing squad, and Aury returned to Galveston—to meet a sharp surprise.

Who had gone there in his absence but two rivals, Jean and Pierre Lafitte, the able pirates of New Orleans. Aury hesitated, negotiated, found his own men drawn to the expert corsairs. His feelings injured, Aury took sail, and the Lafittes gave up the temporary respectability which had followed their part in the Battle of New Orleans and set themselves up at Galveston like hijacking gangsters.

At the long sandy island the Lafittes now created their bizarre Campeachy, a settlement of a thousand or so men and women, not one of them honest, not one with a reputation for dull habits. To Galveston went a crew of renegades, riffraff, violators of many laws of many nations: French, Spanish, white, Negro, mulatto, Indian women, women of a mixture that few could guess at. On the island Jean Lafitte put up a residence-fortress-warehouse, with cannons dominating the surroundings. He named it his Maison Rouge (Red House); others renamed it "Red Hell," for it saw scenes of riot, pillage and wild merrymaking.

Unquestioned king of the crew was Jean himself, directing privateering bands against several nations, but mainly Spain. He told many men, then as before, of his burning hatred for that country. But in later years Spanish records revealed that the Lafitte brothers, like a number of others, were on the King's secret payroll as spies who gave tips against the revolutionists and the freebooters themselves! Here was double-dealing on a broad scale. Eventually the Spanish realized the game the brothers played, but for a long time the Lafittes took the King's money with a smile and a mysterious look.

Before long the loot piled high. To many a planter Lafitte provided hapless Negroes taken from slave ships, though many of his own followers were black or of mixed hues. For a time the lurid spot took on added flavoring, and a touch of tinseled elegance, when former generals of Napoleon arrived with their own men on a mysterious venture that stirred the Spaniards to anxiety and alarm. The Napoleonic element left; the Lafittes stayed.

They were able to carry on as they did for a simple reason: Spain was too weak to stop them. The United States, more and more annoyed at the daring venture, might have been happy to do so, yet Spain feared to admit any kind of American authority over the area. Let the Yankees get one foot on the soil, and they'd take it all. Jean Lafitte made a great demonstration of sparing American vessels. When one of his men moved against a United States cutter, he hanged him, and showed the Americans the body swinging on a tree!

Nevertheless, American resentment grew too strong, and one day in 1821 the officer of an American vessel appeared at Galveston with a serious look and a quiet word. The whole band had to leave. Not taken entirely by surprise (he had spies among the Americans, as elsewhere), the redoubtable Lafitte acted as quietly as his caller and gave in. Not long afterward his helpers set fire to the squalid Campeachy, and all of them left it in smoke.

After that the low, grassy Galveston was deserted for years. During the revolution of the Texans against their Mexican rulers, it became a vital harbor for the Texas navy. What had been good enough for pirates was good enough for Texas patriots. With the founding of the new republic, Galveston served as a major point of entry, with thousands disembarking to join in the surge to the interior or remaining at the strategic spot. The old pirates' retreat was on its way toward rank as Texas' biggest, wealthiest town.

A caller in 1842 found a stir of emigrants, bearers of cotton goods, hard-looking characters, a mixed bag of people and things. Although English was the main language, he heard *buenas dias, bon jour, buon giorno, guten tag, ya ya,* etc, with one or two Indian languages thrown in.

A rowdy Galveston was enjoying American-style prosperity, but meanwhile, down the coast at Corpus Christi, another flamboyant figure had made his debut. He was Colonel Henry L. Kinney, a man who made a career of three- or four-way dealings. The scene was an isolated bay to which one of the earliest Spanish explorers had given its name. Over the years Spain made scant efforts at settlement.

By the 1830s various individuals, smugglers and "traders" of one kind or another, were hovering about the excellent bay of Corpus Christi that was twenty miles across and protected from the Gulf by long islands. The land had something unusual along the Gulf, a sandy bluff forty feet or higher, and its attractions were noted by people who failed to do anything about them. The long lower stretch of land between the Nueces River and the Rio Grande was claimed by Mexico and the United States. This was a situation that offered advantages to a man of nerve and dexterity, and now he stepped forward.

Colonel Kinney was a Pennsylvanian—big, florid, good-looking, an individual of vast adjustability, of extremely private enterprise. He had supposedly courted Daniel Webster's daughter until she said "no," then had gone South to begin a new life in his mid-twenties. Kinney set up a "trading post" in an area whose land he could not own, since Mexico exercised rough control over it. The "trading" that he did was strictly illegal, largely with men who violated Mexican rules.

The Colonel took risks; it was not without reason that, like Lafitte, he put up quarters resembling a fortress and had armed men ready to fight for him. Fight they did, and Kinney fought at their side. For the most part, however, he smiled and finessed his way along. He used joviality, diplomacy—and he also knew when to give payments to the right men in office about him. Soon after his arrival he made a visit of good will to the commander of the Northern Mexican Army, and reached an "understanding." Word spread that people, who wished a minimum of trouble in sliding contraband past the Mexicans, would do well to deal with the colonel.

At the same time Kinney made trips to Austin, then capital of the Texas Republic, and made sure that he also had friends there. The dangers he ran were obvious. At one point a Mexican officer with a land grant in the area arrived with troops and demanded that Kinney get out. Though heavily outnumbered, the master of the "trading post" put on a fake show of strength, so convincingly that the Mexican transferred his grant to Kinney.

The trade of Kinney's many-faceted organization fattened steadily. Whatever happened seemed to help it, and that included war. In 1845, as hostilities over Texas loomed between Mexico and the United States, General Zachary Taylor brought thousands of men to Corpus Christi. Money poured upon the post and its vicinity, and the first effect was immediate: the number of grogshops showed an increase from two to two hundred plus.

One newcomer was not quite impressed. He called it "the most murderous, thieving, God-forsaken hole" in Texas or anywhere else.

The chief of staff spoke a bit less circumspectly. Of the two thousand people who crowded in after the Army, he considered "nearly all adventurers," there to get as rich as they could off the situation. "There are no ladies here, and very few women," he added. Regarding this, Colonel Kinney made a comment which may be recorded as a classic of the Gulf: "Ladies are all right, I reckon, but I've never seen one yet that was worth a damn as a cook."

It was a time and place of street fights, "drunken frolics," "disgraceful brawls and quarrels," of gamblers, shifty traders and crooked ventures. Nevertheless, though few realized it, the shabby spot held an array of future great names of America, including three Presidents of the United States and the only one the Confederacy ever had: Zachary Taylor, U. S. Grant, Franklin Pierce, Jefferson Davis and also Longstreet, Bragg, Sherman and Albert Sidney Johnston.

Then, sadly, the war put an end to Corpus Christi's high doings. After General Taylor led his troops to success, and after the area became part of the United States, Kinney had an attack of the glooms. All those buildings, bars and other establishments, and nobody in them. . . . But, as always, he perked up and tossed before the Americans a real estate promotion with a twentieth-century coloration. He proclaimed this region "the Italy of America," his town "the Naples of the Gulf." He sprinkled advertisements around the country, working with agents in the British Isles, in Germany and elsewhere. Strangers arrived by the boatload and many groaned. Was *this* another Naples? Some went to the interior; enough stayed so that for a while Kinney lacked space for them. Still the colonel went on with "good will" trips, wagon trains to start trade with El Paso and other points. When the Gold Rush began, Kinney advertised Corpus Christi as "the best way to California!" A less raucous population settled here, and a new town was in the making.

By that time another major Gulf center was churning on its way, with an even more daring boom—a grotesque one. Houston grew out of a tall gamble by men who had, above everything else, a cast-iron gall. That it came into being at all is a triumph of will and hope over isolation and mud.

Two separate groups of New Yorkers advanced upon a green, bayou-cut prairie area between Galveston and Corpus Christi. In the 1820s the Harris brothers found a winding, sluggish stream, Buffalo Bayou, which connected with the Gulf, and started Harrisburg, giving it the family name. When the Texans declared their freedom and Mexico's General Santa Anna marched upon them, the

La Lomita: the chapel remains near Mission, Texas

Harrisburgers set fire to their houses and left. Not far off, at San Jacinto, the Texans won their independence when, led by the towering Sam Houston, they routed Santa Anna's forces. The battle lasted eighteen minutes, with 630 Mexicans killed, 208 wounded, the rest taken prisoner, as against nine Texans mortally wounded and thirty less seriously.

The new republic quivered to the name of Houston, and so did another pair of brothers, John and A. C. Allen. In this year of 1836, the Allens had their idea—a new town with the magnificent name of Houston, near the burned out Harrisburg and San Jacinto itself. On paper it was a grandiloquent thing, sixty blocks laid out, a square for public buildings, improvements set out in detail. In reality, this Houston was a large nothing of overflowed prairie and shiny promises. Nevertheless the shrewd Allens went to work, lobbied, and told officials that if they made it their capital, the brothers would give Texas a fine, free city.

The legislators bit, and Houston became Texas' capital before it even existed. One early Houstonian told how several young men heard so much excitement about the place that they decided to see it. "It was hard work to find. . . . When they did, it consisted of one dugout canoe, a bottle gourd of whiskey, a surveyor's chain, and was inhabited by four men with an ordinary camping outfit."

Soon a steamboat—only a shallow-draft vessel could hope to make the trip—was on a maiden journey up the muddy Buffalo Bayou to Houston. It had only passing problems along most of the waterway, with its hanging oaks that dripped Spanish moss and an occasional snake. But the last fifteen miles were a terror, with arms of trees, heavy snags and piles of debris. The crew hacked, pushed and dug their way up the thick ditchlike stream, shadowed by its bushes and vines. It took three days to cover those fifteen miles; several who got out to ride the final stretch in a smaller boat missed the future metropolis, and went several miles too far!

Men stuck tents wherever they could; those who lacked tents slept under thatches, and those without thatches bunked on beds of moss under the skies. When the legislature arrived, its building was not ready, nor were its beds. When John James Audubon paid a call, he found President Sam Houston's mansion a two-room log cabin in muddy disarray, reached by wading in water above his ankles. Nevertheless, for Audubon Houston was a man he would never forget.

For two years Old Sam's Houston remained the homespun cap-

Thriving Corpus Christi: it started as a no man's land

ital of a homespun new nation, and then that rank shifted over to Austin. (Some said that for years the republic had a perambulating capital.) Houstonians shouted; this was unfair, it was tragic. They still lost the capital, and yet the Allens had chosen a good site and had done their job well. Their town grew with the years in a leaping advance that is almost unprecedented in American history.

Houston tapped the rich Brazos River cotton area, a wide hinterland in several directions, drawing lumber, cattle and other products. Houstonians struggled on and on to remove impediments in the serpentine Buffalo Bayou; when a vessel grounded, citizens ran out to help pull it clear. In part the years that followed are a tale of two cities: Galveston against Houston. People of the rival city guffawed at Houston's pretensions to rank as a port; one Galvestonian described it as "the damnedest fake out of doors." When a salt shipment, owned by a merchant named Heidenheimer, melted in the stream, a Galveston paper said with a snicker: "Houston at last has a salt water port. God Almighty furnished the water; Heidenheimer furnished the salt." Still Houston plugged ahead until, in the first years of the twentieth century, there occurred an incident that changed the history of the Gulf, of Texas and, in a certain fashion, of America as a whole. That was Spindletop.

In the early 1900s there was no indication of any pending stroke of destiny about Port Arthur and Beaumont, near the eastern coast of Texas. As late as 1895 Port Arthur had been only a moist waste above the mouth of the Sabine River. Then it came into being, in words attributed to its founder, as the only city "ever located and built under directions from the spirit world," specifically, "the Brownies." Arthur Stillwell, a rich man's son and an unusual one, had the courage of his whimsies. A New Yorker, Arthur had seen his father go broke; quitting formal education in the fourth grade, he worked in a billiard room, became a promoter, earned large sums, bought coal mines and branched out in several other directions. In time he put up the Kansas City, Pittsburg and Gulf Railroad (eventually the Kansas City Southern), but he lacked a Gulf point.

Arthur gambled on hunches, which came to him, he said, from another world, and usually in dreams. As was natural with him, he now communed with "the Brownies," who gave him a precise, detailed plan for a town near the Gulf, with a canal, turning basin and everything else. All Arthur had to do was follow directions, and he did. For this place he knew just the name—his own—and it became Port Arthur.

Into his ventures he drew another less than conventional character, John W. ("Bet a Million") Gates. A Wall street manipulator in the classic pattern, Gates was sometimes embarrassed by his nickname. One story says it became his because, growing restless during a train ride, he watched raindrops roll down a window. To an associate he proposed that each pick a drop and wager a million as to which hit bottom first. His associate lowered the ante to a thousand dollars, but the betting won Gates twenty thousand or more.

"Bet a Million" could win in other ways. Arthur Stillwell decided he needed money for his Port Arthur and Gates agreed to help. Before long Arthur said bitterly that Gates or his aides had helped themselves to Arthur's properties. This time "the Brownies" were of no assistance, and Arthur slipped away in a permanent huff.

A short way off on the coast, Beaumont had a longer history as a quiet lumber town, center of rice cultivation and trapping on the Neches River. Late in the nineteenth century one Pattillo Higgins, a former lumberman, set his eyes on a certain Spindletop, a knoll that rose a few miles out of Beaumont, a mile wide and about two miles long. In the rest of America oil had made something of a splash, and also made people like the Rockefellers. It had yet to be discovered in any vast supplies or to become a common fuel. As for Texas, there had been a few unspectacular strikes, but authorities agreed it would never be found along the coast.

For years local people had noticed the way gas and greasy water seeped up around Spindletop. When the townsmen heard Higgins say that real oil lay somewhere below, they grinned. Poor Pat! He set out a rough town site at Spindletop and named it Gladys City, after a girl he admired. Arguing, appealing, he talked several men into joining his Gladys City Oil, Gas and Manufacturing Company. A drilling was started, another, another; quicksands threw off the drillers, and Higgins subsided.

Along came Antonio Francisco Lucich, from the Austro-Slavic-Italian Mediterranean, who anglicized his name to Tony Lucas. Drawing the interest of several backers, Lucas made new drillings and watched sadly as they brought no result. Were the gigglers correct, after all? Then, on January 10, 1901, a roar broke from deep inside the earth, tossing pipe, tackle and other equipment in the air, smashing the derrick top. The workmen groaned; all that expensive equipment gone. . . .

A moment later, a new roar, and with it a pillar of sickening mud, a surge of gas—and a greasy, greenish liquid. Oil, oil, and so

Spindletop well and monument: where oil changed history

much of it—a flood that went on and on. Tony Lucas happened to be in Beaumont, and when he raced home he saw the dark stuff bathing his crew, his land and his neighbors. One of the latter raged that the "damned mess" was ruining his farm!

For days the oil poured into the air, hundreds of barrels every hour, the noise drowning out every sound, splashing men who covered themselves with hats, goggles, raincoats or anything they could think of. At last, after using levees to hold the liquid, Lucas and his men managed to cap the well. By then Beaumont was America's newest boom town, with thousands riding in, walking in, running in.

They slept in bathrooms, on hall floors, in barber shops, and when they were not asleep they rushed about, asking, trading, making propositions. Farmers were on their way to becoming millionaires in Beaumont, Port Arthur and elsewhere. Great corporations were being formed in hot little cubbyholes, and every kind of thief and swindler was moving around Spindletop. The chief of police issued a locally famous bit of advice: For his own good, let everybody walk in the center of the street after dark, carrying a gun. And let him "tote 'em in your hands, not on your hips, so everybody can see you're loaded."

All of coastal Texas seemed loaded in one fashion or another, and a basic change was in the making for America and for the world. Railroads began to use oil; towns turned to it. Transportation would be revolutionized, and so would machinery and sources of power. Slowly men realized that under the coastal area lay an incredible pool of the fuel, and that America would become its great producer. Jubilee! The word was heard for mile after mile on the Gulf, and new thousands of men and women were to "eat high on the hog."

River Oaks area: Texas' version of the older South

Big,

Bigger,

Biggest

xi

HEART and capital of the western Gulf—eventually to be, it predicts cheerfully, the capital of the coast—is Houston. The city that began so unpromisingly in the mud alongside Buffalo Bayou, has become the surging giant of modern oil, and of a fantastic complex of petroleum-chemical industries that roll swiftly over the area.

Paris is a poet's city; Venice is as picturesque as a teeming stage set; Vienna, San Francisco, New York, Charleston, Boston have particular qualities for which outsiders remember them. As for Houston . . . nowhere else have I, for one, felt quite the throb, the pulsing drive of the place.

For some the town's life has its hilarious aspects; the antics of certain of the "rich-rich" make the flesh of other Houstonians crawl. In a number of circles people talk more constantly about money than in perhaps any other place on earth. Yet Houston has, above all, energy, a free-wheeling, un-southern demonstration of zest and vitality that seemingly never ends, never flags. To visit it for only a few days is to go away exhilarated, or depleted.

A Houstonian, who has only about ten million and is therefore of the medium or middle-class rich, speaks with casual conviction: "You know, this is just about where the country's going to center in the future, and not too far off in the future." In Houston it is not difficult to give full credence to such statements. From its first days the town's growth has been phenomenal; in recent decades it has spurted astonishingly.

As George Sessions Perry noted, in 1850 Houston had hardly one thousand people. Two decades later it counted eight times that number; by 1900 forty-four times as many. Every ten years or so afterward the population doubled. In 1940 it had 450,000 people; it now has more than a million and has jumped over nine other cities to become twelfth in the United States. "You see," the Houstonian says, "that's a right nice start. Now just you wait a while for what's going to come next."

Houston is the country's great oil port, capital and great company headquarters of the industry and everything connected with oil. Enormous refineries cluster about it; wells hum close to businesses and residences and even in the city dump. Oil royalties sprout in highly unexpected and unlikely places. Over the town is the feel, if not the smell, of the sticky black gold, and oil is in the minds and nearly always in the mouths of many Houstonians.

The city is more than oil. Cotton moves out of it in even larger volume than oil; it has the world's biggest cotton firm. As far as it is from the west Texas ranch lands, its county has more cattle than any other. Lumber, rice, half a dozen other products roll through the town in Texas-sized volume. In annual tonnage Houston ranks as the second or third biggest American port, and the largest in cotton exports.

None of this would have been possible, of course, had it not been for Houston's determination to make itself a real port, instead of a bog along the bayou. Year by year its people yanked at snags, sweated to get shallow-draft boats out of the bottom in which they were stuck; they petitioned officials; they did work on this and that stretch, they spent millions of their own. When Washington hesitated to help in dredging, they stepped up with their own cash to assist in the job.

The Houstonians lowered the depth of their channel to eighteen and a half feet, then twenty-five. Only by 1915 did the city get into business as a deepwater port, but today great cargo ships move in and out, sometimes one to an hour. The channel and its vicinity have become a maze of industries, elbowing one another, valued at a billion and a half dollars. For miles there is the rasp of instruments cutting heated metals, the grind of engines, the haze of smoke. Derricks stand against the sky, tanks gleam in the sun, next to herds of cows and an occasional farmer; over the scene swing gulls and herons that fly about this inland seaport.

An easterner, with whom I made an inspection, scratched his cheek. "It's—it's like Pittsburgh . . . with a warm climate."

As he spoke we stared at a curious sight. Gliding along the narrow channel, the great ships appeared to be riding over the land, cutting their way through the grass.

World War II gave an impetus to all this growth, and the years since then have seen its continuation. Houston, the Texas cities to the east (Beaumont, Port Arthur, Orange) and New Orleans as well, are receiving what some call the world's greatest concentration of chemical and petroleum-chemical industries. Natural gas, salt, sulphur, materials for the making of acids, chlorines and alkalis . . . all are here. One industry feeds another, turning over its unused, unneeded by-products to the next, which does the same thing for its neighbor. Here, say the industrial authorities, is the shape of a future America, of a changing world in which the Gulf Coast will have its role. . . .

In the 1850s, according to a story, a friend accompanied Robert E. Lee, then of the United States Army, as they surveyed the Texas plain. Lee seemed to cock his ear, and the friend asked what he heard. "I am listening," said the Virginian, "to the footsteps of the oncoming millions." The millions are there now and more are coming.

But Houston betrays much of its pell-mell development, its sprawling, unplanned, awkward growth. Gleaming chromium and glass buildings lift over the flat plain, and the skyline is a rare sight; yet they may stand next to sidewalk fruit stands and hamburger joints. Drab slums squat at the edges of handsome residential areas with curving roads, fine oaks and magnolias and cypresses. The city has forty-five miles of bayous within its limits, which add to its beauty in many areas, and still, it has never adopted a general zoning system. Even that master of Houston's modern destiny, Jesse Jones, could not swing such a miracle when stubborn "individualists"

RICHARD PERVIN

Houston: it turned Buffalo Bayou into an artery for the nation

HARPER LEIPER

Houston night scene: people once giggled at the idea

Old Sam himself
still rides high

Houston art connoisseur,
studying the subject
outside museum

opposed such routine progress.

Houston is a mixture of places: a port section with boarding houses, supply companies and related enterprises, their names telling of the sea; a section of Louisiana Negroes who still speak some of the French their fathers learned in the Acadian bayou country; a hotel lobby generally filled with cattlemen, recognized by their walk, their high-heeled boots and their talk; a corner occupied by oil field workers; a row of houses of Mexican laborers, a gathering spot for sunburned cowboys from down the coast. And always, too, the homes of the oil rich, the rich-rich, medium-rich and poor-rich, the ones with only a few millions to rub together.

From George Fuermann, historian of the Big Rich, a few tales: A man of oil offered his stout daughter five thousand dollars for every pound she would lose. Another magnate was miffed, when the hotel clerk in a small Louisiana town told him all the rooms were taken. "Direct me to the nearest architect," the injured gentleman said. Even with Texas money an inn could not be finished in a night, but within a year or so he had a place where he could be sure of resting his head when he passed through. A thing like that gives a man peace of mind.

One of the heavily endowed West family, to save time and fuss, parked daily in a bus zone before his office, paying the five-dollar fine, until he had given out one thousand dollars and others complained. . . . At the St. Regis Hotel in New York a barber asked a visiting Texan what he liked to have rubbed in his hair. The Texan couldn't remember. "Phone my barber back home," he said, and it was done.

A schoolgirl, winning a dog in a benefit auction, signed her own check for it, for $110. . . . The Houston *Press* reported that an oil man's wife struggled against a house fire in nightgown, robe and mink stole. The next day her secretary telephoned in a correction: The firefighter had been wearing her marten furs. And the late Jesse Jones, commenting on the once glittering Glenn McCarthy, murmured that McCarthy was hardly a fellow of real stature. "Even *he* doesn't claim to be worth more than twenty million."

Some can be whimsical in their largess. Alvin Romansky recalls a man who has given a limousine to the Star Hope Mission annually, with instructions to drive the local "winos" there in the Cadillac "to lift the poor guys' morale." And the granddaughter of a grande dame caught her breath when the latter, saying good-bye, told her: "Close your eyes. I have something for you." Obediently the younger woman put away the thick roll of bills. Opening them outside, she found herself new-rich in Confederate money.

My favorite Big Houstonian (though not a favorite of many Houstonians) was James Marion (Silver Dollar) West, Jr., one who liked his petty cash to be heavy and shiny. He kept thousands of the cartwheels around the house in racks built for the purpose; his trouser pockets were especially reinforced to hold rolls of them and he scattered them wherever he went, among porters, waiters, children and sometimes plain nonmillionaire civilians, who scrambled like anybody else. As the *Press* commented, "He was to silver dollars what Rockefeller was to dimes."

"Silver Dollar" took his own special butter to restaurants. He liked the color blue, and some said that when they went to his house they might well emerge to discover their cars all repainted in that color. A friend of mine ran into him and was informed that Jim had just received a fine mess of frozen steaks and would send some over. When my friend got home he met a colossal pile of meat, "more than I ever saw outside of a slaughterhouse." Disturbed, he telephoned the master. "Say, I don't have a deep-freeze to hold all that." "Rest easy," "Silver Dollar" calmed him. Soon afterward an enormous locker was delivered. Another telephone message: "I just don't have the place for it in my house." Again "Silver Dollar" signaled for silence; he sent workmen to build an annex to the man's house. The friend was touched. "He was always doing little things like that."

James Marion West had twenty-eight automobiles, more than a third of them Cadillacs. As James Aswell reported, he believed in communication; his house had twenty-five telephones, his garage about ten, and he owned a powerful private radio station. Here his delight in sending and receiving messages merged with the predominant passion of his life: the police. He watched crime with the panting delight of the amateur; he dined with detectives, and long after midnight cruised the city with high police officials whom he joined for raids.

"Silver Dollar," who weighed over two hundred pounds and wore shirts that were more than colorful and ties that matched, had a diamond-studded honorary police badge and a colored, diamond-ornamented belt. He made small presents of a hundred dollars and the like to police officers, playing no favorites, but rewarding everybody of officer's rank on the force. In one cold spell his heart bled for the good fellows, and he gave each of them highly expensive imported coats.

As he rode around he kept his cars—all of which had short wave radio—tuned into police channels. He always carried his own guns. On one burning evening he and a police lieutenant arrested a man reported to be a burglar. There was running fire and one of the lieutenant's wounds came from a .45. In the words of the *Press,* "Both the officer and Mr. West carried pistols; the burglar did not."

All this is, of course, only part of the Houston picture and, many insist, a fading part. There are poor Texans as there are short Texans, Houstonians who look and act like other people, and these last make up the majority. A certain amount of talk about the town's rich-rich is exaggerated there and elsewhere. As many have said, the farther out of Houston a man makes a trip the more staggering a "Texas millionaire" he becomes. And thousands go broke with dry holes or wells that trickle away.

A few arrogant Houstonians have used their vast wealth to "try to buy up the United States," as one critic declared, supporting suspect movements, violent and unstable reactionaries, pouring their money upon candidates in New England and other regions. At times a handful of such men have become a smell in the nation's nostrils. At the same time, many more have used their funds for good, for an astonishing series of educational institutions, amazing medical facilities, the support of a superior symphony. Houstonians back art in a way that, for instance, New Orleans does not. Houston and Dallas lead the South and Southwest in the reading of books. And Houston is acquiring one of the things it needs most: the tempering effect of added years.

From Brownsville, the last point along the Texas Gulf Coast, up to the Sabine and the beginning of Louisiana, there extends a thousand-mile crescent of changing people and changing scenes. First comes the celebrated Lower Rio Grande, "the Valley" to most Texans. That winding river is no enormous stream, but it waters a fertile delta, with carpets of cotton fields and thousands of citrus trees. Date palms, the rich purple of the bougainvillaea, papayas, bamboo . . . These are Texas' subtropics, an area that has sprung up in only fifty years as a cornucopia of winter crops for America.

Mexico lies over the river and the people of Mexico fill much of the valley, as good and peaceful citizens. Some are the tragic "wetbacks," who slip through the water to take any work they can get, and are subject to removal at a moment or a whim. More often the caller finds an air of fiesta, of family parties and redolent chili and

Brownsville: the little girl
behind the iron doors

Brownsville:
market place with
a lingering Latin air

tacos. A line of towns continues in a varying file: Mission, Harlingen, McAllen, San Benito, Edinburg, Mercedes, but the major city is Brownsville.

The Mexican War brought Brownsville into being and it has met a full share of many-sided hostilities. In the conflict with Mexico Zachary Taylor set up a fort which first bore his own name. During a clash in the vicinity the American Major Brown died and the fort took his name. After the war the town witnessed new troubles between the two sides, a number of them beginning when the Latins felt cheated of their land by Yankee politicoes; once a Mexican force took Brownsville in a raid.

During the Confederate War it became an important southern shipping point for cotton and other products, with battles between men in blue and those in gray. Brownsville's location made it a vital rear entryway to the South. Proudly a native told me: "You know Lee surrendered on April 9, 1865. Well, we stayed in the war way later than that. Till May 13, when we had a real fight." Word of the events at Appomattox had not reached the remote area and the Texans killed 115 Northerners.

Up beyond the valley stands the Gulf Coast's major cattle region, a land of sand and mesquite, and also the King Ranch, biggest in the United States, with nearly 850,000 acres and a history of more than a century. Richard King, New Yorker turned steamboat pilot and captain, formed a partnership with Captain Mifflin Kenedy, also of the river. Later the two men separated their enterprises and the King Ranch remains an empire—feudal, jealous of its powers and privileges, basically little changed to the present day.

Grandchildren of families first brought from Mexico by the Kings, live and work on the ranch. Jeeps and helicopters handle cattle under some conditions; scientific farming has been added, and yet the old roundup continues with little alteration. Through the years the King Ranch has pioneered in developing forage grasses, in coping with cattle diseases and in introducing hardy Brahman cattle from India for cross-breeding. By painstaking, minute care the ranch eventually produced the Santa Gertrudis, dark-red, thick, beefy and healthy, the first truly new breed of cattle to be achieved in many years.

Northward lies modern Corpus Christi, a breeze-swept center of cotton, cattle, oil and farming, with beautiful waters, beaches and harbor—and a playground flavoring with a Spanish atmosphere. "Corpus" also has the country's largest Naval Air Station, and tales

Near Rockport: oaks sculptured by Gulf winds

Padre Island: right here the
man say they's a treasure

King Ranch: its Santa Gertrudis cattle are historic

of the somewhat fabulous, sharp-tongued Clara Driscoll. In a hot dispute with the manager of the town's then leading hotel, the doughty lady informed him she would build her own next door, so big she could stand on the roof and spit on his. This, it is said, Mrs. Driscoll did, and today her inn is one of the best appointed for many hundreds of miles.

Beginning outside Corpus Christi is a serpent-shaped stretch of two islands, Mustang and Padre, a hundred and ten miles long, offering a series of beaches, shifting dunes, and a thousand treasure tales. Many men have gone about the sands on many dark errands, and Corpus Christians murmur exciting words: That one buried $100,000 over there, or somewhere nearby. . . . Another sneaked out two heavy chests left by a good old pirate and he's never been seen since. A local organization has even printed a treasure map, telling (roughly) where to dig and for what.

From Corpus Christi extends a file of towns and cities: Aransas Pass, Port Lavaca, Bay City, Freeport, then Houston and Galveston. For generations Galveston has been the play town for hundreds of thousands who have gone there for a relaxed week or weekend, with pleasure places of a dozen kinds and a general air of quiet, or not so quiet, fun. "It's Texas' New Orleans," one Gulf Coaster told me with a grin of happy recollection. "That's what it is, all right," another concurred, but not in approval.

Galveston has known many troubles, many blows. In a fuming dispute over port rates, the town lost a great railroad-steamship combination which went to Houston. Later the line returned to Galveston, but the city suffered. Then, on September 8, 1900, it had the Gulf area's worst single disaster—a hurricane and tidal wave of black memory.

The island lay about eight feet above water. Through that day the Gulf waves lifted higher, higher, the wind moaning ever more eerily. Lower sections of the town began to flood, and people escaped to the mainland or hunted more elevated points. Then it was too late; no one else could get away. A hell of wind and water churned upon them.

In house after house windows broke, walls sagged, and the winds howled so that, though people watched big buildings smash down before them, they could hear no sound. A great wave rolled in; in less than five seconds the level rose four feet more. Men and women were screaming, threshing helplessly about as their homes dissolved around them. Whole sections of land were scooped away; a four-thousand-ton steamship was swept up and dropped on a bank. The wind pulled up trees and thrust them like battering rams through sturdy walls.

Those who found places in which to stay felt them crash around them; those who ran out were choked to death in salt water that came roaring upon them. Roof slates skimmed through the air, and many people had the tops of their heads sliced off by the flying objects. When an orphanage started to give way, each nun tied eight little ones to her, fell to her knees in prayer and pushed into the water. Several of the sisters survived; the rest were discovered later, drowned, each with her charges held to her by the ropes. Death hit everywhere, callously, brutally. No exact count was possible, but six thousand to sixty-five hundred were killed, hundreds of bodies broken, so that they could never be identified.

Dazed, agonized, the town stared at the catastrophe that had struck it. Galveston could not hope to bury the dead who lay on the streets, in trees, or hung out of windows, bloating in the sun. Corpses were put on barges, taken into the Gulf and dropped overboard. But a day later the tides carried hundreds back, spewing out the rotting remains. The survivors made bonfires and burned all they could. In the horror of the situation, many went mad. Disease threatened, looters had a brief spree, and martial law was proclaimed.

Then Galveston went to work with a determination that stirred the nation; some had said it could not come back, yet it did. It erected a powerful seawall of reinforced concrete to keep the waters away; the wall stretched along for nearly eighteen miles, seventeen feet above low tide, with a base fifteen feet thick and granite blocks for a breakwater. Galveston did more: it raised its soil to a new level above the gulf, to the top of the seawall along that area, and in others fifteen feet higher than before.

Just fifteen years after the hurricane of 1900 another hit Galveston, and it stood the blow. Since then it has had other kinds of tests—controversies over politics, gambling and related good-time activities; today it seems headed for a new, more prosperous era. Its natural harbor is one of America's finest, with considerable channel improvement and granite jetties extending miles into the water. It has a calmer air than Houston, its old-time rival, and yet it is a thriving port of cotton, timber, oil and other produce. When its patron figure, W. L. Moody, Jr., died a few years ago, he left an estate of $400,000,000. As a native phrased it: "Mister, even in Texas, that's *money*."

Today, off the coast of Louisiana and Texas, a new future is opening as oil drilling goes to sea. This is a new frontier, an amphibious operation and a dramatic pioneering that have meaning for the world.

Oil workers, riding out regularly in tugs, join a strange life in man-made islands suspended above the rolling waters. On the horizon, out of the fog or against the sun, rise lines of derricks attached to platforms over the Gulf. While authorities of many nations watch the developments, men live here for days in an intricate —at times hazardous—struggle with the elements.

"I never thought I'd turn sailor," a husky member of a drilling crew said, shrugging half in complaint, half in jest. "I'd rather have my two feet on the ground, any time. Still . . ." The work, isolated and unrelieved as it is, cracks tempers and sours dispositions. The men stay out only for short periods at a time, and go back to shore to rest before returning.

The petroleum is there—an estimated ten million barrelfuls, more than a quarter of all American oil reserves. The problem is how to reach it and tap it. Drilling rigs have failed or capsized; some have produced, figuratively, a dry hole in the sea. Everything is more involved, many times more expensive than oil operations in any other place.

To ride out by helicopter, as I did recently, is to see a shoreline sinking quickly into the Gulf, an expanse of choppy blue-green water, and then the rig, like a stylized spider web, reaching toward the clouds. "Easy does it," somebody calls out, and we make a landing far gentler than expected. We are on a platform about the length of a city square, a newly built island that hangs over the choppy waves.

Somewhere beneath us is the silty continental shelf, in which authorities expect to work oil fields as widespread as those already pouring out petroleum in coastal Texas and Louisiana. The sheer proportions of the elevated "island" are the surprise. "The whole thing must go as high as a fifteen-story building," the newcomer ventures. "Nearly twenty, maybe twenty-two," an old hand explains.

As he talks his eyes dart about, scanning a hint of dark clouds in the distance. This is the open sea, in which heavy winds may sweep down in a moment; the drilling companies have learned never to forget that fact. Long steel "legs" extend above and below the platform, which may cost up to five millions, into water one hundred feet deep or deeper.

The platform is a self-elevating one which will sink or rise on order. It has elevators, piles of heavy equipment, engines that drop beneath the surface. When it is finished it may draw up its legs and ride off to the next place. But that will not be for a long time; the hard labor of drilling must continue on and on with little letup.

Down go the complicated mixtures of cement, drilling "muds" and steel casings that will drop thousands of feet into the earth below the Gulf. For days crews will labor and wait, pause and try new combinations, pull up pipes, make changes and then resume. They may have a roaring success or a flat failure, and they will not know until close to the end.

In the night the rigs lift over the dark Gulf, their derricks illuminated by jets of burning gas, and by the yellow lights giving an exaggerated, unreal glare to the whole. Three shrimp boats go by slowly; a plane drones past for a moment; a big fish jumps above the surface, plops away, and there is only the lapping of the water. . . .

Seawall: Galveston lifted itself high for permanent safety

Galveston: the image of the virgin survived the hurricane's fury

Fish, fresh fish from the Gulf!

From Galveston's dock the massive cotton bales are readied . . .

. . . for the lift up and the trip to the world outside

Deepest Gulf Texas: tomorrow we'll be out with the nets again

Still the crews drill on:
portrait in muscle and sweat

Oil refinery: a hum, a throb, a pulsing energy

Offshore wells produce a
tremendous volume of oil

Acknowledgments

OVER a period of years—more intensively during the past four—I have been the beneficiary of acts of kindness and assistance by countless people along the Gulf Coast. Many have contributed documents and volumes, made suggestions and taken me to more remote spots in their localities; others have simply talked and remembered while I listened and learned. Old friends have aided heavily in the collection of data, as have officials, early settlers or descendants, librarians and research authorities in these states and in other parts of the country. In particular I am grateful to:

Ruby Parker and Mrs. Mary Herbert of Pensacola, who sent hundreds of pages of material; Karl Bickel of Sarasota, author of the evocative *Mangrove Coast,* who helped in a dozen ways; Mrs. Gay White, Mrs. Evelyn Rittenhouse and Pressly Phillips of St. Petersburg, who generously gave of time and knowledge.

Caldwell Delaney, author of *Remember Mobile,* and Cameron Plummer of Mobile's Haunted Bookshop; Nash Roberts, for expert advice on weather phenomena; John H. Baker, executive of the National Audubon Society, a friend of other years, who made available the many facilities of his remarkable organization in New York and other sections.

Dorothy Dodd, state librarian, Tallahassee, who provided many leads as to sources; Don Heath, Floyd Martin and W. G. Beach of Houston, who gave prompt assistance with photographic and other data, and Mrs. Dee Woods, long-time director of the Southwest Writers' Conference, Corpus Christi, who loaned out-of-print works.

Alvin S. Romansky of Houston, a lively anecdotist if ever there was one; Tony Ragusin of Biloxi, as informed as he is energetic in the interest of the coast; Marian Murray of Sarasota; Vernon Spencer of New York; Mrs. Henry Gautier of Pascagoula, Mississippi.

Mrs. Edythe Capreol, Beaumont; Fritz Bradley, Tarpon Springs; A. E. Voight, the Oaklands, Bay St. Louis, Mississippi; Mr. and Mrs. Tod Swalm, Sarasota; Mrs. Jo Garland, Key West; Ruby Donahey, St. Petersburg Beach; C. M. Blackford, Homosassa, Florida; Mrs. James M. Robert, Waveland, Mississippi.

Mrs. Merrill Parrish Hudson, Memphis; Walter Hoover and Admiral Whitaker Riggs, Verdun Daste, Jesse Core and John Collier of New Orleans; Bob Aldredge, Beaumont; Kay and Bob McCracken and Katharine Holmes, Corpus Christi; David Westheimer and Margaret

Page, Houston, and Mrs. Lu Hartley Morehead, Long Beach, Mississippi.

Mrs. R. W. Petree, Clearwater, Florida; Ruel McDaniel, Port La Vaca, Texas; Commander Arthur H. Eddins, New Orleans; Judge Anna J. Veters Levy, S. Sanford Levy and Miss Dolly Veters, New Orleans; Stanley Horn, Nashville; Loyal Phillips and Lile Chew, St. Petersburg.

Trezevant Collier, Memphis; Dudley Haddock, Sarasota; Percy Viosca, New Orleans; Ben J. Williams, Promised Land, Louisiana; André Olivier, St. Martinville, Louisiana; Anna Belle Hoffman, Breau Bridge, Louisiana; Mrs. Annie Maude Brown, Pensacola; W. Armstrong Price, Corpus Christi; Bob Sellers, Port Arthur.

A. W. Fisher, St. Petersburg; Edith Dupre, Lafayette, Louisiana; Ted Sumerlin, Houston; Tom McGowan, San Antonio; Robert Conwell, Corpus Christi; Mr. and Mrs. Leander Marx, New Orleans; the late Weeks Hall, New Iberia, Louisiana; Fanny Butcher of the Chicago *Tribune,* and Lloyd Wendt, co-author with Herman Kogan of *Bet a Million Gates.*

Mrs. Edith Amsler, Houston; A. B. Edwards, Sarasota; T. T. Wentworth, Jr., Pensacola; Bob Neitzel, Mansura, Louisiana; Mayor R. B. Meadows, Jr., Gulfport, Mississippi; Arthur V. Smith, Pascagoula; Lindsey O. House, Warrington, Florida; Mrs. Elizabeth Harvey, Pensacola; L. Gibbs Adams and Curt Siegelin, Baton Rouge; R. M. Krebs, Pascagoula, Mississippi.

Robert Meyer, Jr., of Festival Information Service, New York City; S. J. Harrington, St. Petersburg; Fred W. Holder, general manager of Bellingrath Gardens, Theodore, Alabama; Ira Harkey, Jr. and Easton King of the *Chronicle-Star,* Pascagoula, Mississippi; Stanley E. Babb, Galveston News Publishing Company; C. H. Schaeffler, Florida Board of Parks and Historical Memorials; Mrs. Margaret Dixon, Baton Rouge *Morning Advocate,* and Allen Johnson, New Orleans *Item.*

Countess Vera Tolstoy, Alta Loma, California, descendant of Peter Demens, gave kind assistance in clarifying stories about her ancestor.

William Fountaine of Fountaine Library, Columbus, Ohio; Ralph Newman of the Abraham Lincoln Bookshop, Chicago; G. P. Willing, Key West; Jesse Cunningham, librarian, Public Library of Memphis, and Mary Davant of his staff; India Thomas, house regent, and Eleanor S. Brockenborough, assistant, Confederate Museum, Richmond; Herbert E. Kahler, chief historian, National Park Service; Alexander Sprunt, Jr., staff representative of the National Audubon Society, Charleston, South Carolina.

Herbert Evison, chief of information, National Park Service; Byrd Harris, port director, Corpus Christi; Lucia M. Tryon, librarian, Pensacola Free Public Library; Mrs. Margaret Armstrong, librarian, Palmetto Public Library, Palmetto, Florida; Louise Crawford, librarian, and May H. Edwards of the City-County Memorial Library, Bay St. Louis, Mississippi.

Essae M. Culver, state librarian, Louisiana State Library, Baton Rouge; Charlotte Capers, director, Mississippi State Department of History and Archives; Mrs. Miriam G. Reeves, librarian, Louisiana State Department of Education.

Charles M. Brookfield, Florida representative, National Audubon Society; James L. Segrest, chief of division of state parks, state of Alabama, Montgomery; William W. Wells, assistant director, Louisiana State Parks and Recreation Commission.

Virginia R. Porter, librarian, Apalachicola Public Library, Florida; Charlotte Anne Thompson, librarian, University of Tampa; Emerson Greenaway, director, Free Public Library of Philadelphia; Llerena Friend, librarian of the Texas collection, University of Texas, Austin; Frank H. Wardlaw, director of the University of Texas Press; Harry H. Ransom, vice president of the University of Texas.

Joe Templeton, director, Mobile Public Library; Dorothy Traver, acting county librarian, San Bernardino, California; Gloria Brill, branch department librarian, Mrs. Alta Lawyer, branch librarian, Alta Loma unit of the same library; Lucille Bostdorff, reference librarian, Public Library, St. Petersburg.

Mrs. C. A. Service, librarian, Sarasota Public Library; Lucy Stiefel, Dellora A. Gates Memorial Library, Port Arthur; Louis M. Nourse, librarian, and Dorothy B. Neuman, chief, art department, St. Louis Public Library; C. Lamar Wallis, city librarian, Richmond Public Library; Maria Person, librarian, Gulfport Carnegie-Harrison County Library.

Mrs. Cora D. Gautier, librarian, Morgan City Public Library, Louisiana; Mrs. Phyllis S. Burson, librarian, La Retama Public Library, Corpus Christi; and Mrs. Mary Morrow, local history, and James D. Meeks, library director, Dallas Public Library; Mrs. Margaret Pratt and Marie Stanley of the staff.

David Harkness, division of university extension, University of Tennessee, Knoxville; V. L. Bedsole, head, department of archives, Louisiana State University, Baton Rouge; Esther Ann Manion, librarian, National Geographic Society; Milton C. Russell, head, reference and circulation division, Virginia State Library. Mildred Stevenson, reference librarian, Rosenberg Library, Galveston; Mrs. Bessie Schuck, Key West Public Library.

David C. Mearns, chief of the manuscripts division, Library of Congress; John Hall Jacobs, librarian of the New Orleans Public Library, and George King Logan, assistant librarian; Ruth Renaud, Margaret Ruckert, Gladys Peyronnin, Mrs. Alice V. Westfeldt, Marion Mason, Lily Mouton, Mrs. Ellen Tilger and Mrs. Bernice Zibilich of the Library staff.

Dr. Garland Taylor, librarian of Howard Tilton Library of Tulane University; Mrs. Dorothy Lawton, Betty Mailhes, Mrs. Clare Low, Robert

Greenwood, Mrs. Clayre Barr Lewis of the staff, and Martha Ann Peters, formerly of the staff; James W. Dyson, librarian of Loyola University, New Orleans.

Particular thanks go to Frank Dobie, oracle of Texas, who counseled with me on several occasions, and to Mrs. Warren Reynolds, my sister, who worked at my side through all phases of the manuscript, and to Mrs. W. J. Kane and Anna Kane.

Additional help came from Mrs. M. F. Militano, Mrs. A. S. Mitchell and Mrs. Edward S. Sledge of Mobile; Gordon Weel of Miami Beach; Mary Sherard, librarian of the Vicksburg, Mississippi, Public Library; Gratia A. Meyers, librarian of the Carnegie library of Bradenton, Florida, and Gladys Pratt Willing of Key West.

JAMES RICAU expresses his appreciation to those whose help and encouragement made the photographs in this book possible: Mr. and Mrs. James H. Ricau, Sr., Misses Lucia and Cecil Wands, William Pike Bobb, Sr., Mrs. Rita Howard Bobb, Mr. and Mrs. W. P. Langworthy, William C. Richards, John W. Cosgrove, Ethel Edwards, Bernard Rosenzweig, Charles Tudor, Andreas Feininger, the late Weeks Hall, James Edmunds, III, Elizabeth Edmunds, Marian Eames, Dora Thea Hettwer, Nancy F. Genet, J. A. Lloyd Hyde, the late Joseph Woodson Whitesell, T. Labauve, J. L. Baughman, Tobin Armstrong, Joel Daniel, Ben Flint, Eloi Bordelon, the late Joseph Downs, Felix Kuntz, Caresse Crosby, Bernard Cameron, Atkinson Dymock, Mrs. J. L. Thompson, Ruth Haubtman, Elise Bohne, Clement Knatte, Frederick David Bryant, Arthur DiManno, Clair Laning, Norman Thomas DiGiovanni, Arthur LaSalle, Raymond Conner, Howell Edmunds, Michael B. Knudsen, Al Asnis, Hazel McKinley, Henry G. Alsberg, Wayne G. White, the late James S. Edmunds, Sr., Mrs. James S. Edmunds, Sr., Dr. and Mrs. J. D. McLeod, the late Rene C. LaSalle, Mrs. Rene C. LaSalle, Mr. and Mrs. C. S. Kellogg, Dr. and Mrs. Sam Nelken, Mr. and Mrs. James S. Edmunds, Jr., Mr. and Mrs. Austin Reese, Mr. and Mrs. F. M. Hickey, Mr. and Mrs. Wilfred B. Hadley, Mr. and Mrs. William Rhoades, Mr. and Mrs. Grover A. Sheppard, Mr. and Mrs. John K. Tennant, Mr. and Mrs. S. J. McCord, Captain and Mrs. Arthur Spring, Mr. and Mrs. E. M. Frye, Mr. and Mrs. Wayne B. Wands, Sr., Mr. and Mrs. Alonzo G. Enseñat, Mr. and Mrs. Dwight Goodwin, Mr. and Mrs. Wayne Wands, Jr., Mr. and Mrs. Louis Herbert, Mr. and Mrs. William H. Gerdts, Mr. and Mrs. Paul Magriel, Misses Sara, Dorothy and Ada Edmunds, Mr. and Mrs. George Allen Cooper, Mr. and Mrs. William H. Nims, Mr. and Mrs. William Pike Bobb, Jr., Mr. and Mrs. Richard Picton; and to the staff of Compo-Photocolor for professional advice and assistance in many ways: David Mintzer, Kelly Damiani, Ernie Pyle, Richard Schuler, Hans Georgi, Benjamin Morales, Monty Sosa, Romeo Cote, Frank Farino.

In Paris M. Albert Krebs of the Bibliotheque Nationale and Angela Gregory of New Orleans, then in France, assisted me in my use of materials at the Bibliotheque. Captain Robert Estachy of the French Line, New Orleans, and the late Guy Quoniam de Schompre, former French consul here, aided in preparations for study of French collections relating to New Orleans, Mobile and other Gulf Coast localities.

Several hundred books, magazine articles, monographs and other publications were consulted. Particularly helpful were:

ABBEY, KATHRYN T.: *Florida, Land of Change* (Chapel Hill, N. C., 1941).

ARTHUR, STANLEY C.: *Jean Laffite, Gentlemen Rover* (New Orleans, 1952).

BEDICHEK, ROY: *Karankaway Country* (New York, 1950).

BOLTON, HERBERT E.: *Texas in the Middle 18th Century* (Berkeley, Calif., 1915).

BRADY, CYRUS T.: *The Conquest of the South West* (New York, 1905).

CARTER, HODDING, and RAGUSIN, ANTHONY: *Gulf Coast Country* (New York, 1951).

CASTEÑADA, CARLOS E.: *Our Catholic Heritage in Texas, 1519–1936* (Austin, 1936–39).

DOBIE, J. FRANK: *The Mustangs* (Boston, 1952).

DOUGLAS, MARJORY STONEMAN: *The Everglades, River of Grass.* (New York, 1947.)

FUERMANN, GEORGE: *Reluctant Empire* (New York, 1957).

GRISMER, KARL H.: *History of St. Petersburg* (St. Petersburg, 1924); *Tampa* (St. Petersburg, 1950).

HANNA, A. J., and KATHRYN ABBEY: *Florida's Golden Sands* (Indianapolis, 1950).

JOHNSON, CLIFTON: *Highways and Byways of Florida* (New York, 1918).

"Key West and Cuba:" *Bulletin of Pan American Union* (Feb., 1912).

LEA, TOM: *The King Ranch* (Boston, 1957).

LEFEVRE, EDWIN: "Flagler and Florida," *Everybody's Magazine* (Feb., 1910).

MARTIN, SIDNEY W.: *Florida's Flagler* (Athens, Ga., 1944); *Florida During the Territorial Days* (Athens, Ga., 1944).

RIPLEY, ELIZA: *Social Life in Old New Orleans* (New York, 1912).

STOCKBRIDGE, FRANK PARKER, and PERRY, JOHN HOLLIDAY: (New York, 1938); *Florida in the Making* (New York, 1938).

SUMMERSELL, CHARLES G.: *Mobile: History of a Seaport Town* (University, Ala., 1949).

TEBEAU, CHARLTON W.: *Florida's Last Frontier* (Miami, 1957).

WOODS, DEE: *Blaze of Gold* (San Antonio, 1942).

Harnett T. Kane

5919 Freret Street, New Orleans, La.

August 1, 1958

The photographs on the front endpapers of this book are of the monument to the explorer LaSalle at Indianola, Texas and a cannon at Fort Gaines, Dauphin Island, Mobile, Alabama.

The back endpapers show ships at Galveston, Texas and a lighthouse at Biloxi, Mississippi.

Index